# KOP CONTENTS

# Hola . . .

. . . and welcome to The Kop Annual. Many of you may already know and enjoy The Kop Magazine that appears in your shops every month. For those of you that don't know, The Kop likes to mix serious comment with a sideways look at the goings on around the fields of Anfield Road – all in good humour of course. For this one-off 2005 annual, however, we're taking things about as seriously as er, Newcastle's Capital of Culture bid. We've revived some of The Kop's most memorable features, giving them a new slant, and back them up with pages of brand new stuff. The Kop's Heighway Code will point you in the right direction on your travels with the Mighty Reds; you can buy a red scarf or a Rushie muzzy on Lfcbay; test your numbers with the MUFC maths test or take a trip back in time with Erik Meijer. These are just a few of the ideas we've come up with (well what else did we have to do while waiting for Antonio Nunez to make his debut?). So if you don't know what to do with your £8.99, we suggest you take this book to the till and cough up – if you know what's good for you. Either that or make a donation to the 'Igor, Igor, Give Us A Smile' campaign . . .

# INSIDE YOUR KOP ANNUAL:

© Owned by Trinity Mirror North West & North Wales
Limited, trading as Trinity Mirror Sport Media, 2004.

Photographic credits: Liverpool Daily Post & Echo Illustrations: Peter King Production Editor: Paul Dove
Design: Lee Ashun Writing: Chris McLoughlin Publishing Executive: Dan Willoughby
Printed by Scotprint.

# HOLA RAFA!

JULY 2004 and a new boss arrives along with Djibril Cisse – met by taxi driver David Moores at the airport! With Steven Gerrard's Anfield future still very much in doubt, Rafael Benitez had a sombrero for him – and something for Michael Owen . . .

KOP CARTOON

# The LFC Heighway Code

There are a few basics you need to know when you're on the road with the Mighty Reds. Whether you're heading for Rome, Cardiff or visiting the other lot along the M62, you need to know your (Stevie) Heighway Code. Here's the Kop's unique guide to help you on your way

Beware: El-Hadji Diouf on the ball

Warning: This midfield contains Jamie Redknapp

David Seaman in goal (beware chippings)

Warning: Lucas Neill ahead

Likely to encounter England's most successful football club

Hard men at work: May encounter Jimmy Case

Beware: Westerveld in goal at The Riverside

No entry to European Cup trophy cabinet (a sign seen at Chelski and Arsenal)

The road to Hell (assuming you set off from Liverpool)

Welcome to Liverpool

Beware: Kieron Dyer on night out in Newcastle

Florent Sinama-Pongolle and
Djibril Cisse up front

Beware: Squad
rotation

John Barnes
ahead

Beware: Dodgy pitch or
Dwight Yorke's ex-girlfriend

To Goodison Park

Souness era ahead
(no light at end of tunnel)

Fabien Barthez is
lost: Wrong turn

Welsh midfielder's
transfer fee too high

No U-turns (unless
you're Steven Gerrard)

Dennis Bergkamp
free zone

Welcome to Castle
Greyskull

Gary Stevens ahead:
Beware Molby nutmeg

Welcome to
Chris Kirkland's house

Masters 5-a-side

Welcome to Cardiff

Danger: Djibril Cisse
on the run

Matchday
parking zone

**PAUL STEWART**

# Play and win £00,000,000!

# Fantasy Eeeegor

WELCOME to The Kop's exciting and exclusive new fantasy football game.

You've all played fantasy football before and we dare say that one or two of you have even gone against your religion and selected the odd Manc just to try and get the better of your mate at work.

We hope you still felt it was worth dabbling with the devil for that extra clean sheet.

There's no need to think about Mancs, Blues or the Crystal Palace left-back, for that matter, in our game.

This is all about one man and one man only - Igor Biscan.

The game is quite simple to play.

Whatever Eeeegor does this season will earn or lose him points.

But it isn't just about scoring goals, creating chances and keeping clean sheets. There's more to Igor than that.

The points table on this page gives you a breakdown of how our favourite Croat will score or lose points.

So what are you waiting for?

Get playing Fantasy Eeeegor now!

**Booed as sub: -10**

**Eastern European warm-up: +5**

**Sent off/frightened by mascot: -10**

Scores goal in World Cup final: +1000

## How the points are scored

Starting appearance for Liverpool + **2**
Substitute appearance for Liverpool + **1**
Appears in any game after combing his hair + **20**
Scores a goal + **10**
Key contribution to a goal + **5**
Clean Sheet + **3**
Goal conceded -**1**
Hopelessly caught out of position
or skinned for a goal conceded - **3**
Booked - **2**
Sent off - **10**
Smiles + **25 (per smile)**
Surprised at a referee's decision + **1 (per surprised look)**
Has his name chanted by Kop/travelling Kop + **5**
Tries a trick but falls over the ball - **5**
Claps fans when hearing 'Eeeegor'
being chanted + **10**
Does a full eastern-European style warm-up
in front of the Paddock + **5**
Booed when brought on as a sub - **10**
Does a post-match TV interview + **100**
Gets frightened by an away team's club mascot - **10**
Returns to the Croatian international squad + **5**
Gets kicked out of the Croatian international squad
again after returning - **5**
Scores goal in World Cup final +**1000**

All aboard for the **KOP MOLE'S** alternative tour of

LIVERPOOL

Ssssshhh! It's not Paul Ince!

There are many famous locations in the city connected with Liverpool Football Club. From the more obvious to the not so well known, the Mighty Reds' presence can be found in many a nook and cranny. As a special one-off assignment, we allowed the Kop's monthly gossip columnist THE KOP MOLE above ground to take us on a tour of the city's red-hot spots, burrowing for some hidden Anfield gems along the way.

### 1. The Rocket

The Rocket pub at the end of the M62 is one of the first sights to greet many visitors to Liverpool. It's also where you'd find Fabien Barthez on his first day of training at Man Ure. The dozy keeper took a wrong turn and instead of ending up at the Mancs' Carrington training complex, ended up here, asking for directions back to Manchester. The Rocket is named after a train some bloke called Stephenson (that's him pictured below) built and ran on a nearby railway. Of course, that wasn't the only rocket Barthez experienced on Merseyside. He still hasn't seen the one John Arne Riise sent flying past him in November 2001.

### 2. St John's Shopping Centre

We've had many saints (and a few sinners) in Liverpool but perhaps the first - in name at least - was Ian, the striker who scored the winner in our first FA Cup final win in 1965. As his reward, a giant house in Liverpool city centre was built for him. Sadly, he left the club before it was finished so they stuck a load of shops and a market in there instead . . .

### 3. The Albert Dock

Not only did Albert Stubbins make it on to the cover of The Beatles' Sgt Pepper album, he also had a dock named after him in Liverpool. The Albert Dock attracts thousands of tourists every year and numbers have increased sharply since Richard Madeley and Judy Finnigan buggered off to London, thus reducing the chances of bumping into them. Of course, Stubbins isn't the only Liverpool player to have connections with the docks. Back in the late-'90s a dispute saw the Liverpool dockers go on strike long-term and God unveiled a T-shirt after scoring against Brann Bergen to highlight their plight. UEFA weren't impressed and he ended up in the dock with a fine.

### 4. Computer gamestore

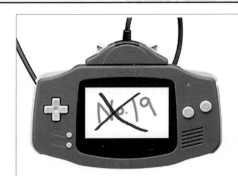

Still around the city centre and we stop off at the shop that played a vital role in us finishing er, fourth in a two horse title race back in 1997. This, indeed, was the very store where David James bought the Nintendo that wrecked his concentration so much that he dropped clangers every week. Judging by his display in Austria for England in September, Sven Goran-Nokia could do with checking his luggage on the next away trip for a smuggled Gameboy.

### 5. Ferri Cross the Mersi

Gerry Marsden's in the wrong business. He should have been a clairvoyant. It was back in the 1960s when he wrote a song for Jean Michel Ferri, a full 30 years before the French midfielder signed for Liverpool. If he knew he was coming that long ago then why didn't he warn us he was going to be crap? Unfortunately Ferri never heard his song get an airing on the Kop – largely because he never played at Anfield before he was sold – and all that's left to remember Jean Michel by now is a boat that was named after him and sails to the Wirral and back several times a day.

### 6. The Backstreets of Liverpool

Footballers hanging round dodgy backstreets in Liverpool make the Sunday tabloids these days but back in 1988, the only thing these lot made was the charts. I'm told that the set for the Anfield Rap video was designed and made by a group of Kopites who learned their trade from professional graffiti artists known as 'Evertonians'. Wonder if Aldo and his mates gave Ron Atkinson his jewellery back?

### 7. The Falcon pub, Kirkby

Some pubs have a trophy the darts team won. Others have a collection of crown green bowling trophies. Phil Thompson's local had the European Cup for a night in 1981. Thommo, who coached the Falcon's footy side, took the trophy Bob Paisley saw more of than his wife into his local after the 1-0 win over Real Madrid in Paris. I can reveal that only one other pub in England has had such a prestigious trophy. George Best's local proudly displays his 1968 European Footballer of the Year award after he traded it in for two pints of Carlsberg and a whiskey chaser . . . allegedly.

### 8. St John's Beacon

Believe it or not, the skyline dominating tower was named after Ian St John by accident. Originally a restaurant, it was a built as a tribute to Ron Yeats and 452 feet above sea level is the same height as Big Rowdy. It was named after St John instead of Yeats when the owners got their Scots muddled up and gave it the wrong name. Radio City now use the tower and the view is so good from up there that John Aldridge does his co-commentaries from there using a pair of binoculars. What was the name of the fella he replaced on the phone-in a couple of years ago again?

### 9. Brick Wall, Croxteth

On the face of it, it looks just like a normal brick wall. But I can reveal that this is a wall of huge historic significance to Liverpool and one which is all set to become a major tourist attraction during the Capital of Culture year in 2008. This is the only brick wall in Croxteth that didn't contain anti-Wayne Rooney graffiti from irate Evertonians following his move to Castle Greyskull. I can also reveal that rumours suggesting there's actually a Sayers in Liverpool where he didn't buy his lunch from are false.

### 10. Stanley Park, Anfield

Spot where Cisse scores winner in 2007 Champions League semi-final v Real Madrid

Billy Liddell statue

No McDonald's

THIS IS ANFIELD.

At least it will be when we've moved over the road to our new home.

But even though the building work has yet to start, that shouldn't stop you from taking a tour of the new place.

On the left is the new Kop, with no sign of a McDonald's, and opposite is the new Priory Road end.

If you look closely you can even see the Billy Liddell statue that was put up after our successful Kop campaign, which began in January 2001, to get the great man honoured. Or maybe not.

And if you go down to the site of the Kop end, you'll be able to stand on the very spot where Djibril Cisse scored the last minute winner in the 2007 Champions League semi-final win over Real Madrid. Whatcha mean we've taken it a step too far now?

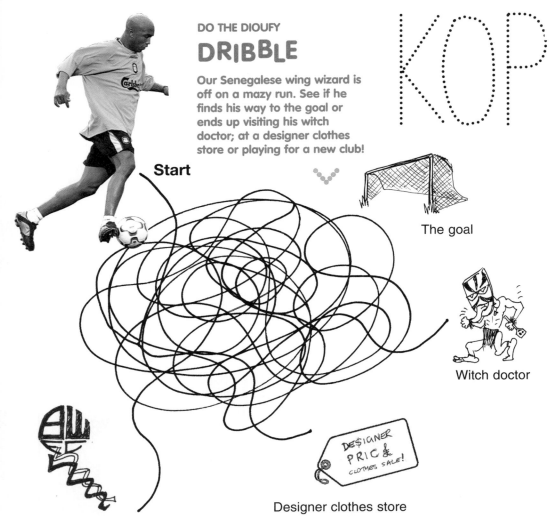

## DO THE DIOUFY
# DRIBBLE

Our Senegalese wing wizard is off on a mazy run. See if he finds his way to the goal or ends up visiting his witch doctor; at a designer clothes store or playing for a new club!

**Start**

The goal

Witch doctor

Designer clothes store

New club

## EL.F.C
# DOT.TO.DOT

Learn Spanish so you can teach Rafa all about our great club next time you bump into him at Anfield. Join up the dots and you will discover the Spanish word for Kop!

## AWAY KIT
# COLOUR IN

Have a guess what colour Liverpool's next away kit will be and colour it in with your crayons!

## FOOTBALL
# ANAGRAMS

See if you can work out the soccer teams and personalities . . .

1. Stained hen rectum
2. Crap alley cats
3. Colin Wanker
4. Lump on arse
5. Nice flares
6. Leaches
7. Go get beers
8. Randy Gay
9. Evil Brazilian afro
10. Pink German beds
11. Beery plastered
12. Defies nude filth
13. Synthetic cream

Answers:
1. Manchester United
2. Crystal Palace
3. Neil Warnock
4. Paul Merson
5. Francis Lee
6. Chelsea
7. George Best
8. Andy Gray
9. Fabrizio Ravanelli
10. Dennis Bergkamp
11. Peter Beardsley
12. Sheffield United
13. Manchester City

## SPOT THE
# DIFFERENCE

A

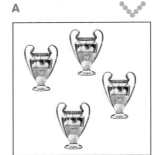

B

See if you can spot the four differences between the trophy rooms at Anfield and Highbury in the two pictures above

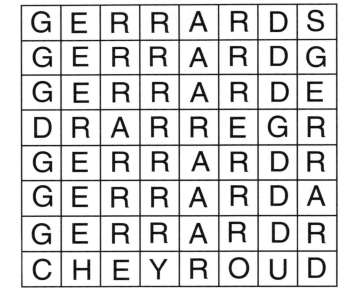

| G | E | R | R | A | R | D | S |
| G | E | R | R | A | R | D | G |
| G | E | R | R | A | R | D | E |
| D | R | A | R | R | E | G | R |
| G | E | R | R | A | R | D | R |
| G | E | R | R | A | R | D | A |
| G | E | R | R | A | R | D | R |
| C | H | E | Y | R | O | U | D |

## MAN OF THE MATCH
# WORD SEARCH

We asked 10 random Kopites to name their man-of-the-match in 10 different games from the 2003/04 season. Can you find all 10 players? They're hidden both horizontally and vertically. Good luck!

OTHER ANSWERS ON
# PAGE 65

Back | Forward | Stop | Refresh | Home | AutoFill | Print | Mail

# LFcbaY

**Anything and everything a Kopite exclusively made-up website and been promising yourself. Here's just**

| **All Items** | **Auctions** | **Buy It Now** |

football magazine            Sporting Goods

☐ Search title **and** description

---

### CAMEROON GRASS  Bids: **1**  Time remaining: **7hrs 14mins**

**Authentic grass, staple diet of international African footballers – and Toxteth terrors**

As eaten regularly by Rigobert Song at Melwood and during Mersey derby celebrations by a Mr R. Fowler

---

### BUD LABEL  Bids: **0**  Time remaining: **9hrs 42mins**

**Authentic Bud label (bottle not included) worn just once by Don Hutchison as unique posing pouch**

Ideal for the young footballing gentleman to protect his modesty while in a state of extreme undress on a night out in town. Slightly stained and torn. As seen on video

---

### ROONEY'S VEST  Bids: **0**  Time remaining: **15hrs 55mins**

**Vest with words 'Once A Blue, Always A Blue' written on**

Formally owned by an 18-year-old who is now living in Manchester. Would suit person making hollow show of loyalty to 35,000

---

### WOK  Bids: **3**  Time remaining: **17hrs 4mins**

**Cast iron Chinese cooking implement able to withstand hot temperatures**

This multi–functional item not only cooks but was once used as an ironing board by a Mr Peter Beardsley – who found it got the creases out of his shirts perfectly

---

### 90 MIN STOPWATCH  Bids: **2**  Time remaining: **21hrs 4mins**

**Stopwatch, well worn and not in best condition owing to previous owner's occasional fits of bad temper**

Bidders should be aware that this time-piece seldom mirrors time in the real world. May be stuck on Castle Greyskull time. Genuine bidders only – no time wasters

---

### TURNTABLE  Bids: **12**  Time remaining: **1day 10hrs**

**Once owned by Emile Heskey, similar to the invisible model seen on rare celebratory occasions in the L4 area**

New manager has the team playing to a different beat, these hit and miss turntables no longer in use. Available for quick sale at knock–down price – just like former owner

---

🌐 Internet zone

wants can be found on Lfcbay. Just log on to our bid for that red scarf or Heskey turntable you've a few of the items that are on sale . . .

click here)

**Search** Refine Search

### CUT-UP SHOES
Bids: **0**     Time remaining: **19hrs 14mins**

**Stylish brogues, size 13, bought by a Mr Ruddock now in pieces after accident while in transit**

Severly damaged footwear could double as sandals. Heels well worn due to the weight they've carried and can occasionally leave a trail of blood in their wake

### FINNISH MULLET
Bids: **1**     Item withdrawn

**Stylish '80s hairpiece, as sported by Finnish striker who has now moved out of area**

A Mr L.Garcia, who has recently moved from Barcelona to Merseyside, has now purchased this mullet

### RED SCARF
Bids: **7**     Time remaining: **15hrs 55mins**

**An ideal present for your schoolteacher at Christmas. Well worn. Perfect for walking through storms**

Scarf has state-of–the–art global positioning system built in. Apparently the previous owner was forever turning corners in his

### CLEAN SHEET
Bids: **3**     Time remaining: **17hrs 4mins**

**A common sight at Anfield in 1978-79**

A Mr Clemence has one of an unrivalled collection of 28 from this unique era up for sale

### NEW HOMES MAG
Bids: **2**     Time remaining: **8yrs 42days**

**1995 guide highlighting homes in Merseyside area. Not used, good as new**

Proves beyond all doubt that the North West lacks housing comparable to the scenic West Midlands area of Cannock – eh Stan?

### NOSE PLASTER
Bids: **12**     Time remaining: **1day 10hrs**

**Breathe-easy nose strip as worn by God himself**

Product helped God to perform miracles on a regular basis. Not been used for a while, may have lost some of its magical powers

.

# MUZZY marvels

No self-respecting Liverpool legend from the glorious past would be seen on the town without one. We are, of course, referring to the much maligned furry lipwarmer. The muzzy was a compulsory fashion accessory in years gone by. But who had the best one? We pitted a couple of 'taches against each other to see who would trump who – and we reveal our star card . . .

**Liverpool**

**The "Johnno"**

| Style: | English Gentleman |
|---|---|
| Colour: | Chestnut |
| Bristle: | 55% |
| Celeb double: | John Cleese |
| Scouse rating: | Sound |

**V**

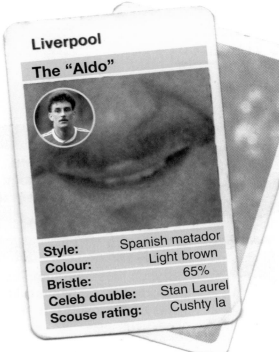

**Liverpool**

**The "Aldo"**

| Style: | Spanish matador |
|---|---|
| Colour: | Light brown |
| Bristle: | 65% |
| Celeb double: | Stan Laurel |
| Scouse rating: | Cushty la |

**Result:** The John Cleese factor beats Stan Laurel and there's not much to choose in the colour and bristle factors but The "Aldo" nicks it in this clash of the local Anfield hitmen

**Liverpool**

**The "Brucey"**

| Style: | Big game hunter |
|---|---|
| Colour: | Light brown |
| Bristle: | 45% |
| Celeb double: | Manuel |
| Scouse rating: | Grobbelaar-ey |

**V**

**Result:** Only one winner when these two meet. Brucey's knees would be wobbling for real if he came up against the might of the Magnum. Even Yosser Hughes was a fan . . .

**Liverpool**

**The "Magnum"**

| Style: | Hollywood Love Rat |
|---|---|
| Colour: | Sandy brown |
| Bristle: | 77% |
| Celeb double: | Magnum |
| Scouse rating: | Gizza job |

**Liverpool**

## The "Lawro"

| Style: | Greek kebab seller |
|---|---|
| Colour: | Medium brown |
| Bristle: | 68% |
| Celeb double: | Bob Carolgees |
| Scouse rating: | Ooh la, la ...la |

**V**

**Result:** Warky first invented the 118 look but Lawro's Scouse factor (plus classic '80s mullet) is boosted by his likeness with Mick Quinn, er, sorry, Bob Carolgees. Lawro just shaves this one.

**Liverpool**

## The "Wark"

| Style: | 118 118 |
|---|---|
| Colour: | Fair/ginger |
| Bristle: | 65% |
| Celeb double: | Burt Reynolds |
| Scouse rating: | Aye, aye |

**Liverpool**

## The "Barney Rubble"

| Style: | Traditional centre part |
|---|---|
| Colour: | Dark brown |
| Bristle: | 62% |
| Celeb double: | Charlie Chaplin |
| Scouse rating: | Avin' a Barney |

**V**

**Result:** 'The Barney' may have looked the Real deal in Paris '81 but the 'Rushie' is one half of a perfect double act (with Aldo of course). To me, to you, to you, to me . . .

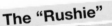

**Liverpool**

## The "Rushie"

| Style: | Greyhound owner |
|---|---|
| Colour: | Light brown |
| Bristle: | 73% |
| Celeb double: | Barry Chuckle |
| Scouse rating: | Boss, la |

**Star card:** The Kirkby kid who started it all is the ace in the Muzzy Marvels pack. Topped off with a curly perm, Macca invented the trademark Anfield look. While others were combing their bum-fluff outside the offy, our Teh was making life hairy for Anfield opponents. R-e-s-p-e-c-t.

**Liverpool**

## The "Terry Mac"

| Style: | Calm down, calm down! |
|---|---|
| Colour: | Who's askin? |
| Bristle: | 88% |
| Celeb double: | Harry Enfield |
| Scouse rating: | You startin? |

MUZZY marvels

✍ IS it true that some members of the Finnish Liverpool Supporters Club paid a visit to Anfield in January, 1980?

I can vaguely remember some odd-sounding fans loitering outside the old souvenir shop after one match.

I'd be grateful if you could solve this for me as it's been bothering me for some time now - 24 years to be exact.

*G. Otnolife,*
*Diehard Red*

**A: Yes, that is in fact the case as our picture (above right) proves. I believe they were 'odd-sounding' because they were speaking Finnish, although I cannot confirm this.**

✍ I BUMPED into a Jari Litmanen lookalike in our local newsagents. He was buying 20 Benson & Hedges and a packet of extra strong mints. Do I win a prize?

*Brian Straw-Clutcher,*
*Hants*

**A: No.**

✍ I REMEMBER Tommy Smith once wearing a sombrero. Do you think he knew about the Spanish 'Rafalution' long before anyone else did?

*Marty McDonnell, Donegal*

**A: Our picture (below) confirms your suspicions. Wonder if he knows what's going to win the 2.30 at Uttoxeter tomorrow?**

✍ I FOUND an old autograph book in my attic the other night and was astonished to see the great Alex Raisbeck's name printed with a Bic biro. I now believe this to be a forgery as such writing tools were not in circulation until at least the 1950s.

*Via e-mail*

**A: Bad luck, a cruel hoax.**

✍ ACCORDING to a neighbour who is a keen twitcher, Liverpool's original sponsor was going to be Birdwatcher's Weekly and not Hitachi but they pulled out of the deal when they discovered that there's no such living creature as the Liver bird?

Is this true?

*D. Aftbloke,*
*The suburbs*

**A: No. And whaddaya mean there's no such thing as a Liver bird? I saw two on top of a very tall building on Liverpool's seafront as I drove past just this morning.**

✍ HAS Liverpool's carrot-topped former no. 12, who put that French side to the sword with a last minute winner some years ago, ever been on safari in a TR7?

*Via e-mail*

**A: Yes, see the photo, right.**

✍ I HAVE spent weeks making a model of Anfield using discarded cereal packets, toilet rolls and empty Pot Noodle cartons. I have also used an old knitting needle to reproduce the look of the historic Kop flagpole. If any readers have any unwanted astroturf, could they send it on to me as I believe it will double perfectly for grass and I can paint on the pitch markings with some Tipp-ex I have found in an old pencil case.

*A. Norak, Suffolk*

**A: Is Luton near you? I believe they may have some left over from the 1980s when it was regularly used as a top-flight playing surface by clubs not good enough to win on grass.**

✍ NOW that Michael Owen has gone, is it safe to return to my seat just to the right of one of the goalposts at the Kop end?

I left because I was afraid of getting hit (or having my flask of coffee knocked over) every time the Anfield Boy Wonder took a penalty.

*Pen Alty,*
*Carshalton*

**A: I don't think Michael can expect the Galacticos faithful to be as understanding as you regarding his very occasional waywardness from the spot. And to think - they've got Beckham to put up with too, so no-one is safe in the Bernabeu!**

✍ AFTER some years of searching and giving up hope on ever finding it, I have finally found the winning ticket for the Year's Free Supply of Kop snack bar Wagon Wheels competition in 1982. Am I too late to collect my prize?

*Ron Sad, Croxteth*

**A: Yes.**

✍ I AM writing with my left hand after regretfully coming to blows with a (former) friend and long-standing fellow Kopite, so please excuse my handwriting being below the expected standard in fans' correspondence.

The reason for our argument is all too familiar. He said that former Anfield number seven, Kevin Keegan, the great Mighty Mouse, once got hit in the face with the ball and a nasty-looking bruise prevented him from boarding the plane on one of Liverpool's European trips.

I said that he was mistaken for a prank that the ex-striker played with an orange and that he did in fact board the plane.

Can you please prove me right by publishing a photo from your extensive archive that will settle this argument once and for all so we can get on with supporting Rafael Benitez' Spanish revolution as friends once again?

*A. Jaffa, Southport*

**A: Your scuffle and subsequent writing concerns were well worth it - you have won the argument as our picture, left, proves all too well.**

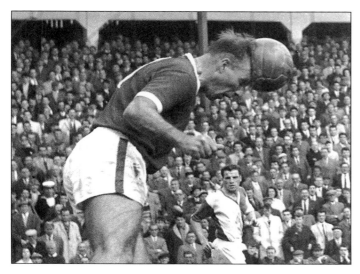

✍ I AM sure there must have been occasions in the past in our beautiful game when match balls have not been pumped up to their regulation pressure.

Whilst I make every effort to monitor the matchball tension while watching from my regular seat in the Upper Centenary Stand, as you may appreciate this is not always as scientifically foolproof as I would like it to be.

Can you help?

*E.G.Head,*
*Widnes*

**A: This ball (see picture above) looks rather flat having landed on former Liverpool star Ronnie Moran's head like the proverbial pancake while Blackburn star Stig Inge Bjornebye looks on.**

✍ IT'S a known fact that if you play Black Sabbath records backwards you can hear the devil talking. Is it true that if you play 'The Anfield Rap' backwards, John Aldridge sounds really posh?

*R.M. Odla,*
*Looprevil*

**A: No!**

✍ IT'S about time Joey Jones got some recognition for being a modern man. To sample frogs legs in the '70s (the age of meat and two veg) was very brave and adventurous. Not to mention his willingness to experiment in the kitchen, making native Swiss desserts. And gosh, he was even chewing on the Bavarian feast of Gladbach that I still can't to this day find in any cookery books. Hats off to Mr Jones.

*Mrs D. Smith,*
*Norfolk*

**A: Stick to what you know love, and forget about the football.**

✍ HAVE you any photos of former Anfield great Ian Callaghan in cabaret while wearing a straw boater? My wife would love to see this as Ian is one of her all-time favourites. Thank you.

*Andy Williams,*
*Litherland*

**A: Only too happy to oblige (see below).**

✍ I HOPE you can solve something that's been troubling me. I regularly go to the Kop and my favourite song is the 'Fields of Anfield Road'. However, I've been living in the Anfield area for many years and I've never known there to be any actual fields on Anfield Road. On the contrary, it has always been quite a built-up area. With this in mind, perhaps we should rename the song 'The Streets of Anfield Road'.

I'm also sceptical about the line 'where once we saw the King Kenny play' as the only place I've seen Dalglish ply his trade is actually inside Anfield - with not a field in sight! I hope our fans can rectify these historical oversights.

*Ed Eagle-Eye*
*(86 years old), Anfield*

**A: Two points well made Ed.**

## KOP TIPS ... KOP TIPS ...

\* **Brought to you in association with the bloke that made that giant Crown Paints tin that used to sit in the centre circle before kick-off in the 1980s**

\* *GIVE yourself more room to celebrate a goal in style by standing outside the ground instead of sitting in your usual seat. When the crowd cheer loudly, feel free to wave your arms wildly and run down the road without fear of being reprimanded by Anfield stewards.*

**Dave 'Shanks' Pony,**
**St Helens**

\* *RECREATE the spirit and unforgettable passion of the old Spion Kop by simply rolling up an unwanted copy of the Echo and urinating through it on to an adjacent spectator.*

**Soft Lad, Kirkdale**

\* *GET yourself a Terry McDermott perm for free by unplugging your bedroom lamp and sticking your fingers in the socket.*

**A. Calm-Down, Walton**

\* *MAKE a nuisance of yourself in the pub before a game by pretending to be Mark Lawrenson.*

**M. Lawrenson, London**

\* *RECREATE the look of that classic Candy kit of 1989/90 by wearing your usual Liverpool shirt and standing under a pigeon-infested building on the city's waterfront.*

**R. Lars, Allerton**

\* *DRY out your Echo by simply spreading the soaking pages on a nearby radiator on the ward.*

**Soft Lad, Fazakerley Hospital**

\* *I'VE discovered a foolproof way of getting into the match for free every week. Unfortunately, however, I can't tell you how as it's a secret.*

**Ian, St John's Ambulance**

\* *ATTRACT Rafael Benitez' attention in the dugout by wearing a Spanish sombrero and shouting 'My mother is unwell,*

*can you give me directions to the beach' in his native tongue.*

**Carl Los, Mertheythide**

\* *MAKE yourself feel wanted by changing your name to John Arne Riise and then standing to acknowledge the chanting crowd when Liverpool win a free-kick.*

**Billy No-Mates, Liverpool**

\* *GET in free for Sky games by sticking two dead tarantulas to the back of your hands and pretending to be a TV presenter.*

**Dicky Kees, Liverpool**

\* *MAKE yourself a Kop legend by clinching the Double with the winner at Stamford Bridge in your first season in charge as an Anfield player manager.*

**K. Dalglish, Anfield**

\* *HAVING scrambled eggs for breakfast? Spice things up by inviting half of the Liverpool squad and backroom staff. Hey presto, you've got instant Spanish omelette.*

**Adi Ohse, Leeverpool**

\* *SMUGGLE stilts in to the match and when fans sing 'Stand Up If You Hate Man U', they'll know you REALLY mean it.*

**Mr Manu-Hater, Anfield**

\* *IMPROVE Channel Five's coverage of Liverpool by taping it on long-play and then playing it back on short-speed and enjoy listening to John Barnes at normal speed.*

**Otto Kew, Berlin**

\* *IF you find yourself caught in Nazi gunfire, don't pop your head out of the bunker.*

**Scouser Tommy,**
**South Africa**

\* *WHEN you walk through a storm I find it helps if you hold your head up high.*

**Howard Gail, Wavertree**

# THE KOP SHOP

This game of **Frustrating** will have you tearing your hair out. Hours of fruitless dribbling will drive you mad!

Ooooooooooooohhhh Gary! Annoy your mates with this **Helium Pundit Balloon** that sounds just like the real thing. Let the air fly out and listen to those squeaky pearls of wisdom from Lawro!

Ever wished you could beat the Blues every time? Well now you can with Rushie's **BLUEBUSTERS!**

**Hong Kung Eric** – number one fighting Manc! Enjoy hours of fun with this mini martial arts toy that will jump into unnecessary and explosive violent action when prompted by verbal abuse from a complete stranger.

First marketed in eastern Europe but now gaining popularity in Britain – especially in Liverpool where model is earning cult status. Permanent look of surprise guaranteed every time with the **Ginger Eeeegor.**

This **Barney Rubble** cuddly toy comes complete with two European Cups and Liverbird on chest.

ACTION DAN

Everyone's favourite **Action Dan.** Take Dan to Castle Greyskull and watch him score the winner time after time. Now available in London.

Darren Anderton's **Operations** game – enjoy hours of fun playing the surgeon as you try to put Sicknote back together again.

It's the European version of **Collect Four**. See if you can help Sir Alex get those elusive four Cups.

This bad-tempered horse will kick out if he doesn't get his own way – better make sure you let **BuckaRuud** win!

Based On The
**Russia's beautiful game**

Who cares about loyalty to your club when you can sign up to Chelsea and become a **Billionaire!**

Ssssssssssssshhh! Don't wake the sleeping **Furgy,** 'cos once you do he won't stop chewing an' ranting 'til he's red in the face. If he sees an opposition Furgy he doesn't like, expect a few choice words. Over 18s only due to foul language. You have been warned.

StevieG

The **Stevie G moneybox** – no matter how much cash you put in, he'll stay a Liverpool super hero!

# Anne-field Frank's KOP
## Dates to Remember 2005

**WELCOME. TO HELL MY ARSE! IF YOU WANT A SHELL TRY THE GRAFTON ON A FRIDAY NIGHT**

## JAN

3 years since - Jamie Carragher injured 13,706 Arsenal fans at Highbury with a single coin that he returned to the stand after it was thrown at him. The last few victims are due to be released from hospital by the end of this year. 6 years since - Liverpool beat Southampton 7-1 at Anfield with all seven goals coming from Academy graduates in the shape of Robbie Fowler (3), Michael Owen, Dominic Matteo, Jamie Carragher and David Thompson. Bet it never happens again. 17 years since - Liverpool announced they had signed a £1 million three-year shirt sponsorship deal with Candy. How come they never put a washing machine in the centre of the pitch before kick off like Crown Paints' big tin?

## FEB

5 years since - Members of the Merseyside Branch of the Liverpool Supporters Club successfully lobbied the Government to make February 31st 'Sir Alex Ferguson' day. 101 years since - former Liverpool outside-right Dick Edmed was born in Kent. Have we ever had a player with a better name?

## MAR

1 year since - Pele included El-Hadji Diouf in his list of 125 greatest living players. At least Pele proved his sponsors' slogan of 'There are some things money can't buy but for everything else, there's Mastercard' to be correct. Clearly you can't put a price on Pele's stupidity. 3 years since - the legendary 'Welcome to hell my arse. If you think this is hell you should try the Grafton on a Friday night' banner was unfurled at Galatasaray's notorious Ali Sami Yen Stadium. Class.

## APR

4 years since - Phil Mitchell got shot and, so the BBC could show it in its usual time slot, Liverpool's UEFA Cup tie with Barcelona in Spain was put back. Sadly, he survived. 18 years since - Gary Ablett scored his only goal for the Reds against Notts Forest at Anfield. And they say Brian Clough was a football genius. 21 years since - Dennis Law sent the Mancs down to Division Two with a cheeky back-heeled winner for Man City at Castle Greyskull. He retired the day after as a Maine Road legend.

## MAY

1 year since - Former Liverpool reserve Trevor Birch was appointed as Everton chief executive. Bill Kenwright described him as having 'a far-reaching understanding of football'. 13 years since - Mark Wright shouted 'You f***** g beauty' in front of the Dutchess of Kent after receiving the FA Cup. She was pleased with the compliment. 78 years since - Newcastle United last won the championship. No wonder Freddie Shepherd thinks it's the

## JUN

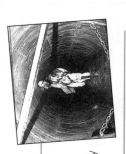

3 years since - El-Hadji Diouf tied Frank Leboeuf in knots during Senegal's shock 1-0 World Cup win over France. He later went on to screw another Frenchman over; this time for £10 million. 12 years since - Nigel Clough was signed from Notts Forest for £2.75 million.

## JULY

1 year since - Former Liverpool reserve Trevor Birch resigned as Everton chief executive. Clearly that 'far-reaching understanding of football' came in useful and he got out as quick as he could. 18 years since - An old Victorian sewer collapsed underneath the Kop (right) and rebuilding work meant the Reds had to play their first three games of the season away from home. Given that Kopites used to just p*ss down a rolled up Echo back then, they probably collapsed through lack of use.

## AUG

2 years since - The Kop Magazine celebrated its 100th edition. As part of the celebrations we received a telegram from Lizzie of Buckingham Palace, launched a campaign to get Kenny Dalglish knighted and received many plaudits, except from Ian St John who described it as 'the worst in living memory'. 19 years since - Luton Town banned away fans from watching their odious team on their plastic Kenilworth Road pitch. I still hate them now. 23 years since - Liverpool paid Middlesbrough £450,000 for David Hodgson. Steve Gibson is still seeking an extra £437,890,000 for him as they had to knock down Ayresome Park and move to a new home over a decade later and it was all Liverpool's fault.

## SEPT

31 years since - Liverpool's record 11-0 victory against Stromsgodset in the European Cup Winners Cup at Anfield. Brian Hall and Ray Clemence were the only players not to score. Good job Gerard Houllier wasn't in charge really or we'd have sat back at 1-0 and tried to hold on. 117 years since - Everton played Accrington Stanley in Anfield's inaugural Football League game. Who are they? And does anyone know what Accrington are up to these days?

## OCT

5 years since - Kevin Ratcliffe said Nick Barmby 'deserves everything he gets' during his first Merseyside derby for Liverpool. Presumably he hadn't meant a goal in a 3-1 win. 38 years since - Former Liverpool captain Paul Ince was born. After retiring from football Ince is expected to follow Eric Cantona into the movie business. He's already been lined up to star in 'The Ego Has Landed'.

## NOV

2 years since - Djimi Traore scored for Liverpool with a right-footed effort in rain-soaked Bucharest. Romanian air-traffic control later reported being asked by several pigs for permission to land at Bucharest airport. 23 years since - We played the Toffees for a laugh and left them feeling blue, 5-0. One, two, one two three, one two three four, 5-0. Rush scored one, Rush scored two, Rush scored three and Rush scored four, nah, nah, nah, nah, nah, nah, nah.

## DEC

7 years since - Gerard Houllier came up with his famous 'five-year' plan during a late night Christmas Eve meeting at Anfield. Since then Liverpool have turned 41 corners, had 22 blessings in disguise, won 6 trophies, beaten Everton 4 times at Goodison, signed 3 Englishmen and sacked one French manager. C'est la vie. 38 years since - Gary Sprake threw the ball into the back of his net at Anfield as Liverpool took on Leeds. The Kop sung 'Careless Hands'. Why didn't we sing that for David James instead of 'England's number one'? 41 years since - Gary McAllister MBE was born. His birth certificate says 'Motherwell' but judging by his displays at the end of the treble season 'a stable in Bethlehem' would be more realistic . . . as good a place to end the story of 2005 as anywhere!

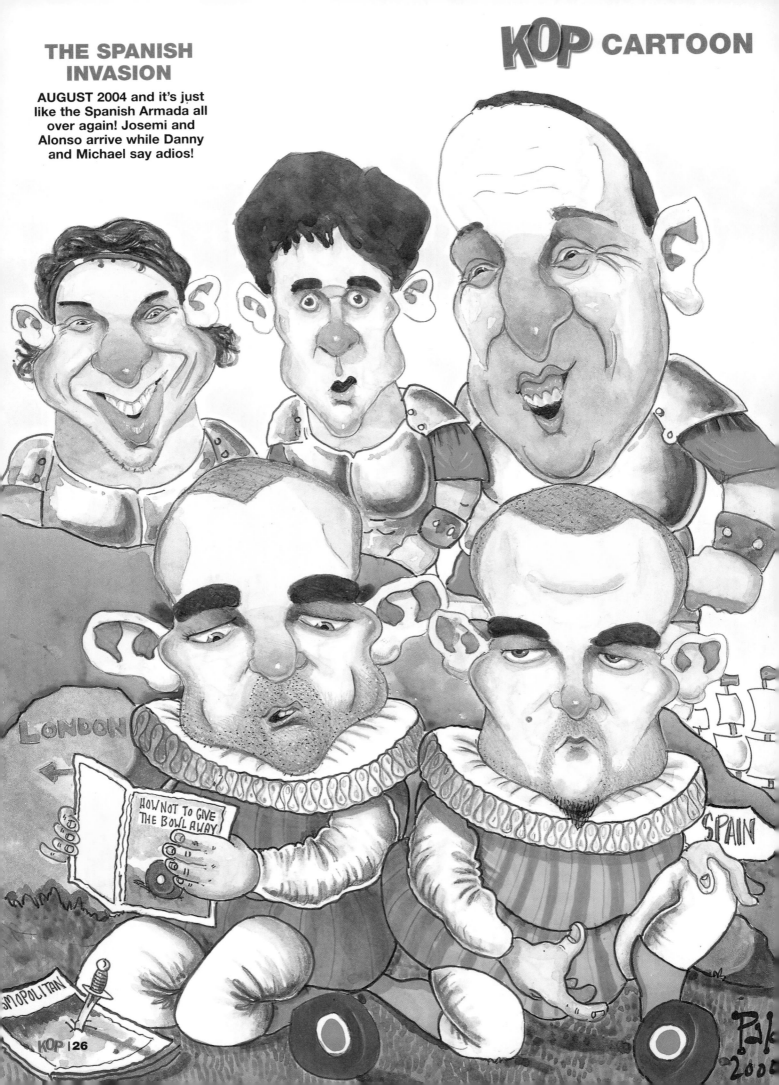

THE SPANISH INVASION

AUGUST 2004 and it's just like the Spanish Armada all over again! Josemi and Alonso arrive while Danny and Michael say adios!

KOP CARTOON

*This is to certify that on July 27, 2004
an historic event in the illustrious history
of Liverpool Football Club did occur*

*namely that*

# Stephane Henchoz

*in the Rentschler Field Stadium, East Hartford,
Connecticut, USA did
score with a right-footed volley
in the 62nd minute of Liverpool's 5-1
victory over Celtic in the Champions World Series*

**Also in this series: The 'Rob Jones hit the post' and 'Djimi Traore scored from 35 yards' certificates. Coming soon: 'Carra's hat-trick' and the day 'Real Madrid Were NOT Linked With Any Of Our Players'**

## Shooting for the Sky with Shearer
*(With apologies to Lennon and McCartney, written after Newcastle's Champions League qualifier exit in 2003)*

Picture yourself at a spot in Newcastle,
With bare-chested Geordies and
half-eaten pies
The referee whistles, you step up quite slowly,
The Champions League is in your eyes.
Patrizan players of the old Yugoslavia
Standing with hands on their heads
Looks at the ball with the goal in his eyes
And it's gone

(Chrous) Shooting for the sky with Shearer,
Shooting for the sky with Shearer,
Shooting for the sky with Shearer

Follow the ball past the bridge
and a Quayside
Where Newcastle players get

drunk and crash cars
Everyone smiles as it drifts past the Boro
It's well on its way up to Mars
Newspaper headline appear the next morning,
Waiting to have their own say
Leant too far back, now the ball's
in the clouds, and it's gone.

(Chorus) Shooting for the sky with Shearer etc

Picture yourself on a plane in the airport
With long delays 'cos of pens in the skies
NAC Breda are next at the turnstile,
Those Geordies with tears in their eyes

## Yesterday
*(With yet more apologies to Lennon and McCartney, written for Gerard towards the end of the 2003-2004 season)*

Yesterday,
All my troubles seemed
so far away,
Now I need fourth place
if I'm to stay
Oh, I believe in
yesterday

Suddenly,
We're not half the team
we used to be
There's a shadow
hanging over me
Oh, yesterday came
suddenly

Will I have to go?
I don't know,
I couldn't say
I signed Salif Diao,
now I long for
yesterday

Yesterday,
We were not an easy
team to play,
Now I wish O'Neill
would go away
Oh, I believe in
yesterday

Mm mm mm mm mm.

# KOP Karaoke

SHOOTING WITH SHEARER

YESTERDAY

OH DANNY BOY

**If there's one thing about The Kop, it's that we like a good sing-song.
We all know the traditional favourites like YNWA and The Fields of Anfield Road but we like to spice things up every month with**

## Danny Boy
**(With apologies to half of Ireland and everyone else who's sung it . . .)**

Oh Danny boy, your gripes, your gripes are boring,
From the Redmen, down to a London side,
Liverpool's gone, and all we hear is whining,
'Tis you, 'tis you must stop slagging Rafa's side.
But come ye back when Charlton's up at Anfield,
Or when you're hushed and not having a go,
'Tis we'll be here in sunshine or in shadow,
Oh Danny boy, oh Danny boy, we loved you so.

## Wayne Rooney in a Brothel
**(with apologies to Christina Aguilera)**

If you wanna be with me,
Baby there's a price I'll pay,
I'm Wayne Rooney in a brothel,
Eighty quid for all the way.
If you wanna be with me,
I can make your wish come true,
I'll sign autographs while waiting,
I like anything that's blue

I'm Wayne Rooney in a brothel baby etc

## I Think We're On Loan Now
**(With apologies to Tiffany, written during 2003-2004**

Children won't play
That's what he says when we're at Melwood
He sent us away
We're not in demand
And so we're

Sent on loan as fast as he can
Thankfully not up to Sunderland
Trying to get a game
at somewhere s***e
And if we don't do something special
We'll come back and get sold
Like Stephen Wright

I think we're on loan now
There doesn't seem to be
any Reds around
I think we're on loan now
Trying to prove ourselves in
half-empty grounds

Look at the way
Alou got sent to France forever
Vignal's now in Spain
And no-one knows what
happened to Mellor

Sent on loan as fast as he can
Can't get a game down at West
Ham, Semi's at Bolton,
now wearing white
And Babbel's stuck at Blackburn
Even though we're having
problems down the right . . .

## Two Thousand and Four
**(with apologies to the Fab Four again, written on a bad day in 2004)**

When I was younger and I had hair,
Years ago from now,
Bill Shankly was putting out a super side
Big Ron Yeats and Thompson out wide,
If I'd got there at quarter to three,
They had locked the door,
The Redmen won easy, why can't it still be
Nineteen sixty-four.

Went down to Wembley, to win the cup,
Just before Shanks left,
Super Mac was shouting
that the Mags were best,
Keegan scored two, Newcastle
undressed.
Kop choir singing, flags in the air
A Scouse victoree
The Redmen won easy,
why can't it still be
Nineteen seventy-four.

We were the greatest,
we'd never lose,
We were number one,
You'd have to be a
player to get in the side,
World's best team was
on Merseyside.
Winning the treble,
victory in Rome,
Who could ask for more?
The Redmen won easy,
why can't it still be
Nineteen eighty-four.

Now that I'm older,
pulled out my hair,
Glory days have gone,
What on earth has happened
to the Liv'pool way,
Our great clubs
wasting away.
Passing and moving,
playing football,
Gone for evermore?
Now we're not
top three,
why must it now be
Two thousand
and Four?

a few alternative words put to various tunes. So here's a few examples from our Anfield Arms night out when we necked a few Kop cocktails and stepped up to the mic. Did we regret it the morning after? Er, you decide . . .

I THINK WE'RE ON LOAN NOW

ROONEY IN A BROTHEL

TWO THOUSAND & FOUR

**ISTVAN KOZMA**
**Hungary and
Liverpool**

# Manchester United Football Club
# Maths
## examination

*Pupils should answer all questions. The exam will last for 90 minutes plus any additional time needed to ensure a good result for candidates who are at home. Pupils forgetting to provide a sample (of their rough work) will be punished with a lengthy ban from the school team.*

1. Rio is very forgetful. One morning he is asked to stay behind after training to take a drugs test but he forgets to take it and goes home where he forgets to answer his mobile phone. As a result, the FA aren't very happy with naughty Rio and threaten to punish him. Please express.

a) How long he will be banned from playing football.
b) How many England players Gary Neville will try and persuade to go on strike as a result of the ban.
c) Rio's IQ (to one significant figure).

2.

Alex has won it once, Bob has won it three times. Alex has one, Bob does not. What are we referring to? Please explain your answer (because no-one else can).

3. Ryan is a Welshman. Express, as a percentage:

a) The number of friendly internationals he has missed through injury on a Wednesday night before recovering to play for Man Ure the following Saturday.
b) The number of major international football tournaments he has played in since his Welsh debut.
c) The amount of his total body weight that is made up by his chest hair.

4. Mr Riley is a referee from Leeds. In the 2002/03 season he officiated in four games at Castle Greyskull and awarded them six penalties, plus one at Goodison Park. What percentage of Ruud van Nistelwar's goals that season came from assists by Mr Riley?

5. If Castle Greyskull holds 67,000 fans on a matchday and 3,000 of those seats are set aside for visiting supporters, please explain:

a) How many prawn sandwiches are munched on average during the half-time interval?
b) How many decibels higher is the noise from the visitors' section in comparison with the rest of the ground?
c) How many pins could you hear drop after Robbie Fowler scored twice there for Liverpool when away supporters were banned due to building work?

*Sory — I
Fourgot
Luv Rio*

6. Jose is a Portuguese national who brought the team he formerly managed to Manchester in March. Please answer the following questions:

a) How many minutes of injury time did the Russian referee fail to add on to allow a late winner after Costinha scored to knock United out in the 90th minute?
b) At what mph did Jose run from the bench to join his players in celebrating his side's late goal in front of the travelling supporters?
c) How many objects were thrown from the stands at Jose after he held both of his middle fingers up to the Stretford End as he left the playing area at full-time?

7. How many more times have Manchester United won the European Cup than Nottingham Forest?

8.

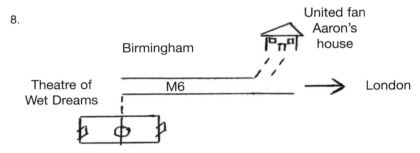

Aaron is a loyal Manchester United supporter and travels to see all of their home games. How much quicker does it take him to get home on a matchday now that the M6 Toll Road has opened?

9. Gary isn't very popular on Merseyside. At what angle did he raise his hand while in order to make rude gestures towards the travelling Kop after a late FA Cup goal at Castle Greyskull in 1999?

10. Ruud is a Dutch centre forward who happens to look like a horse. Express, in metres, how long his face is.

11. Alan is from Leeds. He used to play for his local team but has now moved to Manchester to play for a new team at a cost of 6 million dirty Mancunian dollars. He scored 56 goals in 228 games for Leeds and received 60 bookings. Please answer the following questions.

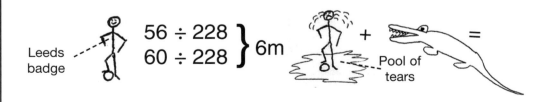

a) Express as a percentage Alan's bookings per game ratio compared to his goals-per-game ratio for Leeds
b) How many times did Alan kiss the Leeds United badge during his X seasons at Elland Road? (Put your answer to the nearest thousand)
c) How many of the tears he shed after Leeds got relegated could be described as 'crocodile'?

*DON'T TELL
ME WHAT
TO DO!
— KEANO*

12. Mikael is a French defender who spent the summer in Portugal. How many penalties did he manage to give away during Euro 2004 and what page of the new edition of the Guinness Book of Records will you soon find him on?

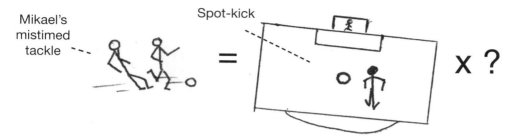

Mikael's mistimed tackle

Spot-kick

= x ?

13. x = 94 y=17 z = £7.5 million. Please work out the following equation. If x is equal to Diego Forlan's appearances for Manchester United, y is equal to Diego Forlan's goals for Manchester United and z is equal to the amount Alex paid Independiente for his services, by how many million has z been over-valued?

14.

Cristiano

Visiting defender

Ruud

10 yards

If a visiting defender at Castle Greyskull runs within 10 yards of Cristiano and another visiting defender runs within 10 yards of Ruud at precisely the same time, which one of them hits the turf first?

15. Roy is 45 yards away from the referee at Castle Greyskull, Gary 32 yards away and Alan 27 yards away. If Roy can run at 22mph, Gary can run at 17mph and Alan can limp at 2mph, which one of them will stick their vein-bulging forehead in the ref's face first, presuming Gary doesn't stop to verbally abuse the nearest Scouser on the way?

16. Alex and Gordon are both Scottish. Alex, a football manager, can manage 232 swear words every 90 minutes. Gordon, a chef, can manage 246 swear words every 90 minutes. How many swear words would be heard if the pair of them spent half-an-hour together?

Foul-mouthed Scot Alex

Youse are all f**!&*g *!!**@** and you can **!!@ &*&** **£!&** !!** and ***! *^&!! * **!!@

Foul-mouthed Scot Gordon

Call that a f**!&*g omelette? You can *!!**@** and you can **!!@ &*&** **£!&** !!***^&!! **!

17. Eric used to play football for Manchester United. He is now an actor in France. Please answer the following questions:

a) Please express, in inches, how much bigger Eric's waistline is since he retired from playing football.
b) How many more chins than Gary Pallister does Eric now have?
c) How many millions does Eric still make from appearing for a couple of seconds in every advert Nike make despite having as much involvement in football now as ITV Digital?
d) How much money, in pence, has been made in box offices across the world from Eric's films?

# INVISIBLE HANDS-FREE POGO STICK

Hit unparalleled heights with this ground-breaking new product from the people that brought you the life-size Bill Shankly miniatures and the Anfield Legends' Breath in a Jam Jar series.

**STUN** your work colleagues with the extra **BOUNCE and VITALITY** you get from the **INVISIBLE HANDS-FREE POGO STICK** – and enjoy the **FREEDOM** of being able to use the rest of your upper body for those **MUNDANE CHORES** that so often leave you **ROOTED** to the ground.

**SIMPLY** pogo into the air at home, surprising your family when **LIVERPOOL SCORE** and frustrate your **NEIGHBOURS** by **REBOUNDING** off the ceiling at record speed with an **IMPRESSIVE** crunch.

This unique product has also been approved by the PFA – the Pogo-jumping Football Association – so you can enjoy the benefits of **EXTRA BOUNCE** the instant you step on to the football pitch. **RISE** above your opponents at corners and **BE NOTICED** first as you **TOWER** above other customers at the bar for that post-match drink.

Alternatively, finish those jobs you've been meaning to complete for years by reaching damaged **ROOF GUTTERS,** rotting upstairs **WINDOW FRAMES** and overgrown **GARDEN TREES** without the use of a **LADDER.**

So, don't hesitate! Simply write to the address below, enclosing a cheque for an **UNFEASIBLY LARGE AMOUNT OF MONEY** to this never-heard of before address: **INVISIBLE HANDS-FREE POGO STICK OFFER,** 12 Made-Up Street, Madeup Town, Nowhere and get the extra bounce that you've always wanted **NOW!**

*Please note: No guarantee can be undertaken as to the invisibility of the product. Cheques are non-refundable.*

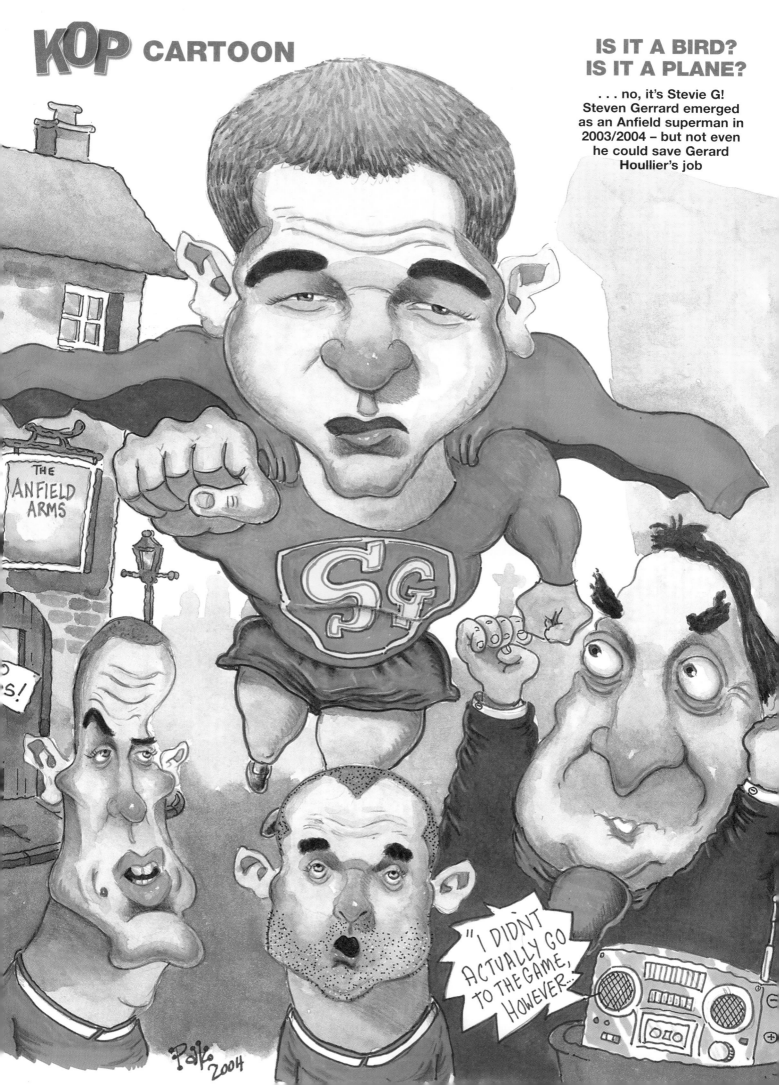

Back  Forward  Stop  Refresh  Home  AutoFill  Print  Mail

## Not found what you want yet on
## Here's a few more Anfield items
## Anyone for an old Rushie muzzy

**All Items**  |  **Auctions**  |  **Buy It Now**

football magazine | Sporting Goods

☐ Search title **and** description

---

### BOX OF TISSUES, OPENED
Bids: **4**   Time remaining: **30 mins**

**This is the very box of tissues with which Harry Kewell wiped away the pain of his wife's passing on Emmerdale**

The first and second boxes were opened and finished before Emmerdale got to the adverts but this third box is available for sale, only partly used

---

### RUSHIE'S MUZZY
Bids: **0**   Time remaining: **9hrs 42mins**

**Make a bold fashion statement with this perfectly coiffered top lip warmer**

Ideal for storing food on long car journeys. It may also cause Evertonians severe discomfort

---

### INVISIBLE BRICK
Bids: **11**   Time remaining: **15hrs 55mins**

**Boffins believe it was this very invisible brick which Mark Walters used to step over 150 times a game**

Bidders be warned there are Auxerre supporters who have placed a price on the brick's head. In later years, stepping over it became a problem for the previous owner

---

### PEGGUY'S LUCKY CHARM
Bids: **1m**   Time remaining: **17hrs**

**Nothing has ever brought one team so much good luck (or six trophies in six games)**
**Priceless**

It was the lucky charm, not the lucky player, that saw Liverpool perform cup heroics. Rafa Benitez doesn't look like he'll need luck to bring success to the Kop

---

### BRUNO'S BOOTS
Bids: **2**   Time remaining: **21hrs 4mins**

**Bruno Cheyrou's white boots. Perfect condition, hardly used**

Otherwise known as footballing Kryptonite. Previous wearer found all his powers and talents drained whenever he pulled them on, forcing sale

---

### RIISE CHEST RUG
Bids: **12**   Time remaining: **1day 10hrs**

**Genuine JAR chest hair, collected from the owner's bathroom floor**

An ideal alternative to spray-on-hair for the topless ginger gentleman. No reserve price, although stocks are running low.

## our unique Kop auction website?
## up for sale if you make the right bid.
## or some genuine Riise chest hair?

click here)

 Search  Refine Search

---

### FRAMED GOAL PICTURE    Bids: **45,000**   Time remaining: Eternity

Action picture of the occasion when Rob Jones finally found the net for Liverpool

This empty picture frame will require dusting. Also included with item is giant box of torn betting slips

*Picture not available*

---

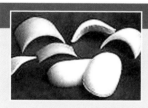

### SHOULDER PADS Bids: **0**    Time remaining: **9hrs 42mins**

Comedy shoulder pads tailor made for dodgy coloured 80s' suits

**NO RESERVE**

Long-haired previous owner Mr Venison no longer given television air-time forcing the reluctant sale of these items. Suits already with charity shops

---

### BABB CREAM    Bids: **7**    Time remaining: **15hrs 55mins**

Endorsed by Phil Babb for use after serious mishaps with goalposts

Has excellent pain killing qualities although it cannot hide embarrassment

---

### No. 20: SUB'S BOARD    Bids: **1 (Mr R. Evans)** Time rmg: 20 hrs

Well worn substitutes board held up seemingly during every match. Roy never let Stig get too tired

The opposite of Igor's current situation. Stig never lasted 90 minutes, subbed with a few minutes to go all the time. Igor can't get more than 90 seconds

---

### VLADI'S NUMBER 7 SHIRT    Bids: **1**    Time remaining: **7hrs**

Went missing at the start of the 2003/04 season and hasn't been seen since

Largely worn August to May from 1999 to 2003, although was often unused for months on end during that period. Comes with weight of history, likely to attract bids from Australia

---

### GARY MACCA SHAMPOO    Bids: **12**    Time remaining: **1 day**

Unused gift for supremely talented Scotsman who excelled at Anfield

Offered to Paco Ayesteran but he politely declined, now available to Reds' supporters

# Sir Bob's photo album

We all know him as Sir Bob. The most successful British club manager in history. His haul of three European Cups while in charge at Anfield will surely never be surpassed. As a special tribute to Paisley, we're taking a glance into his photo album with a few doin's an' that from the loveable genius himself. How he would have hated all the palaver . . .

*We're on the Heighway to heaven with Bob's Reds*

*Great cross that!*

**School days, just like his Anfield career, ended in Honours**

*Match that, Mrs Ferguson!*

*That's four European allotment trophies for Jessie now*

**The ability to be better than the rest ran through the Paisley family**

Walking the touchline at Anfield on match day, Sir Bob glimpses a tough guy Hollywood actor in the dugout. As if the Reds needed a hard man with Jimmy Case and Graeme Souness in their side!

*I don't remember putting thingymebobs Pacino on the bench . . .*

Rome, 1977 and a momentous occasion in Liverpool history.
If only Keegan hadn't left the roll-on Brut in his hotel room,
it would have been the perfect night

Paisley continued the Anfield
evolution started by Shankly

Scouse boxing legend John
Conteh was also bowled over by
Sir Bob's charm

# Sir Bob's photo album

When the Prime Minister asked for his autograph Bob popped the question

A young Scottish upstart appeared on the scene, thinking he knew it all

A brew-up in the bootroom was always welcome - unless Souey was around!

One day there was a chance meeting with Good Morning Britain presenter Nick Owen in a local kebab shop

In times of trouble, it was always good to turn to Shanks for advice

Sir Bob met the odd yard dog in his time . . .

Sir Bob was a dab hand at talent spotting to keep spirits up on the Kop

There were no big 'eds and no job was too small at Anfield

At the end of the day, a sing-song was usually in order when another trophy landed on the Anfield sideboard

# KOP TV guide

## MON

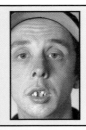

**9am Big Brother:** Phil sets Gary his weekly task of going seven days without having a pop at Scousers.

**10.15am Teletubbies.** Mark Viduka, Jan Molby, Micky Quinn and Big Nev attempt to shed a few pounds by running up Teletubby Hill. With guest appearance by Neil Ruddock.

**11am Memory Bank:** With Rio Ferdinand.

**11.01am Two Pints of Lager and a Packet of Crisps:** Ex footballers talk about their diet. With George Best.

## TUE

**9am Big Brother:** Day 2 and it gets ugly in the house after Gary fails his task. * May contain unpleasant images.

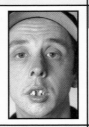

### DOCUMENTARY

**10.15am Cutting Edge.** A review of how Gerard Houllier's tactics put opposition teams to the sword at Anfield during 2003-2004.

**1pm Talking Balls:** Elton Welsby is joined by Mark Lawrenson.

**2pm Mind Your Language:** With Peter Reid and Alex Ferguson. This week, Ron Atkinson joins the class.

## WED

**9.30am Pet Rescu:** Find out whatever happened to Chelsea's Romanian full-back, Dan.

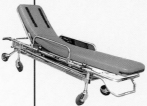

**11am Casualty:** A look back at Bryan Robson's career (repeat).

**2pm FILM: Mission Impossible.** Alex Ferguson tries to surpass Bob Paisley's three European Cup wins.

## THUR

**3am Sex and The City:** A look back at Leicester's trip to Malaga.

**9am Bread:** The Nevilles star in Bread.

**10am: Bargain Hunt:** Join Leeds boss Kevin Blackwell in his search for players.

**11am FILM The Nutty Professor.** Starring former Leeds chairman John McKenzie.

**5pm Blue Peter:** Peter Kenyon's guide to contracts he prepared earlier.

**6pm Christmas Grotto:** With Ken Bates and Abel Xavier.

## FRI

**10am Top Gear:** Jamie Redknapp and friends discuss their wardrobe.

**10.15am House Doctor:** This week the house doctor rushes to treat Richard Wright after he falls out of his parents' loft and tells the tale of Thomas from Norway, who suffered a nasty injury getting out of the bath.

**2.30pm Red Dwarf:** A look back at Paul Parker's career at Castle Greyskull.

**2.40pm FILM: Clueless** Mike Walker's guide to managing a big football club.

## SAT

**11am Channel 4 Racing From Haydock Park:** Can Ruud van Nistelwar win the Diving Dutchman Maiden Stakes?

**10.15am Eastenders.** Julian Dicks gets ready for pre-season training with a couple of Big Macs and a pint down the Old Vic.

**5pm Buffy the Vampire Slayer:** Buffy takes on Jim Leighton.

## SUN

**11am Praise Be:** Liverpool fan John Paul gives thanks for the glory of Rome.

### KIDS CHOICE

**9am Brat Camp:** A look back at trophyless Irishman David O'Leary's time in charge of his young babies at Leeds.

**6pm The Muppet Show:** With Arsenal's fans.

# From Bryan Robson in Casualty and ugly goings-on in the Big Brother house to Jamie Redknapp's Top Gear and the Weakest Link with Bjorn Tore Kvarme and Gary Ablett, it's everything you need to know about what will be on the box in the next seven days!

**7pm Subbuteo World Championship:** With commentary by Pat Nevin and Tony Cottee.

**8pm FILM: Gone in 60 seconds.** Highlights of England's Euro 2004 clash with France.

**1am Hell's Kitchen:** Various Premiership players show what they will be roasting this Christmas.

## PICK OF THE DAY

**8pm FILM: Dirty Harry** Leeds United fans give their opinions on Harry Kewell.

**10pm Restoration:** David James surveys the ruins of England's Euro 2004 campaign in Portugal and Big Dunc plans his latest comeback.

**12.30am Loos Women:** With Rebecca Loos.

**1am FILM: I Know What You Did Last Summer.** With David Beckham, Posh Spice and Rebecca Loos.

**7.30pm Keeping Up Appearances:** The unlucky Chris Kirkland attempts to go a full month without missing a game through injury.

**9.30pm The Royle Family:** Fly on the wall documentary. This week can the family find a big enough hat for Joe to wear?

**10pm Cold Feet:** Steven Gerrard talks about a move to Chelski.

**1am FILM: I Still Don't Know What You Did Last Summer.** With David Beckham and half of the women in Madrid.

**7pm I'm A Celebrity Get Me Out Of Here:** With Urs Meier, Jeff Winter, Pierluigi Collina, Graeme Poll etc . . .

## KICK OF THE DAY

**8pm The National Lottery:** Where will David Beckham's next penalty kick end up?

**3am Home and Away:** Soap opera. Where has Dwight Yorke been playing this week?

**5.30pm Happy Days:** Newcastle United fans talk about the glory years at St James' Park. Features actual footage from the 1950s.

**8pm A Place In The S*n:** With Graeme Souness and Wayne Rooney.

**9pm FILM: The Never Ending Story:** Newcastle United's search for silverware continues.

**11pm The X-Files:** Series looking at footballers and their past romances. This week Caprice talks about what she saw in Tony Adams.

## MISS OF THE DAY

**6.30pm The Weakest Link:** Igor Biscan and Djimi Traore battle it out for a place in the Liverpool defence, along with previous winners Bjorn Tore Kvarme and Gary Ablett.

**8pm Fantasy Football:** How Arsenal won the European Cup.

**9pm FILM: 101 Dalmations** Stan Collymore goes dogging.

**10.30pm FILM: Minority Report.** A look at the number of Man Ure fans in Manchester.

**8pm Location, Location, Location:** Kirsty and Phil try to find a new place on the cheap for a 126-year-old Merseyside Football Club who are desperate to move from their ageing home.

**9.30pm FILM: City Of The Living Dead.** Filmed on location at the Riverside Stadium, Middlesbrough.

**6am-10pm FILM: From Dusk Till Dawn** A look at how often you'll hear TV ads featuring a Clive Tyldesley voiceover on a daily basis.

*'And who can forget that glorious night in Barcelona . . .'*

# Liverschool Timetable:

Head Teacher: **Mr Benitez**

| | 9am – 10.15am | BREAK 10.15am – 10.30am | 10.30am – 12pm | 12pm – 1pm LUNCH | 1pm – 2.15pm | BREAK 2.15pm – 2.30pm | 2.30pm – 3.30pm |
|---|---|---|---|---|---|---|---|
| **Monday** | MATHS Learn to count missed chances. Teacher: **Mr Heskey** | BREAK | DOUBLE SCOUSE. Teacher: **Mr Molby** | Menu: Pie, Chips, mushy peas, gravy. Head of canteen: **Mr Dicks** | GEOGRAPHY. Italy – like living in a foreign country? Teacher: **Mr Rush** | BREAK | BIOLOGY. Sex education. Teacher: **Mr Diouf** |
| **Tuesday** | MUSIC: How to write a dodgy rap. Teacher: **Mr Johnston** | BREAK | ENGLISH (DOUBLE). Teacher: **Mr Dalglish** | Menu: Pie, Chips, gravy. Head of canteen: **Mr Dicks** | RE. How to 'go fourth' like God said. Teacher: **Mr Houllier** | BREAK | IRISH. How to speak to an Egyptian official on a touchline. Teacher: **Mr F*****g-Aldridge** |
| **Wednesday** | PSYCHOLOGY. Teacher: **Mr Shankly** | BREAK | MIDWEEK ASSEMBLY. Trying to turn a mess into success. Led by: **Mr Benitez** | Menu: Pie, Chips, mushy peas, gravy. Head of canteen: **Mr Dicks** | HISTORY. The barren years, 1991-1994. Teacher: **Mr Souness** | BREAK | WOODWORK. How to use pine in DIY. Teacher: **Mr Thompson** |
| | COOKERY: How not to deal with spices. Teacher: **Mr Evans** | BREAK | TREBLE EUROPEAN STUDIES. Teacher: **Mr Fagan** | Menu: Pie, Chips, mushy peas, gravy. Head of canteen: **Mr Dicks** | ECONOMICS. How to pass round a pound. Teacher: **Mr Ruddock** | BREAK | PE. Severe physical punishment. Teacher: **Mr Ayesteran** |
| **Thursday** | GEOGRAPHY. A guide to conquering Rome. Teacher: **Mr Paisley** | BREAK | DOUBLE CHEMISTRY. Teachers: **Mr Gerrard and Mr Alonso** | Menu: Pie, Chips, mushy peas, gravy. Head of canteen: **Mr Dicks** | HUMANITIES. When to go topless in public. Teacher: **Mr Riise** | BREAK | ART: The art of goalscoring. Teacher: **Mr Fowler** |

LIVERSCHOOL

RAFA... WAS ERE

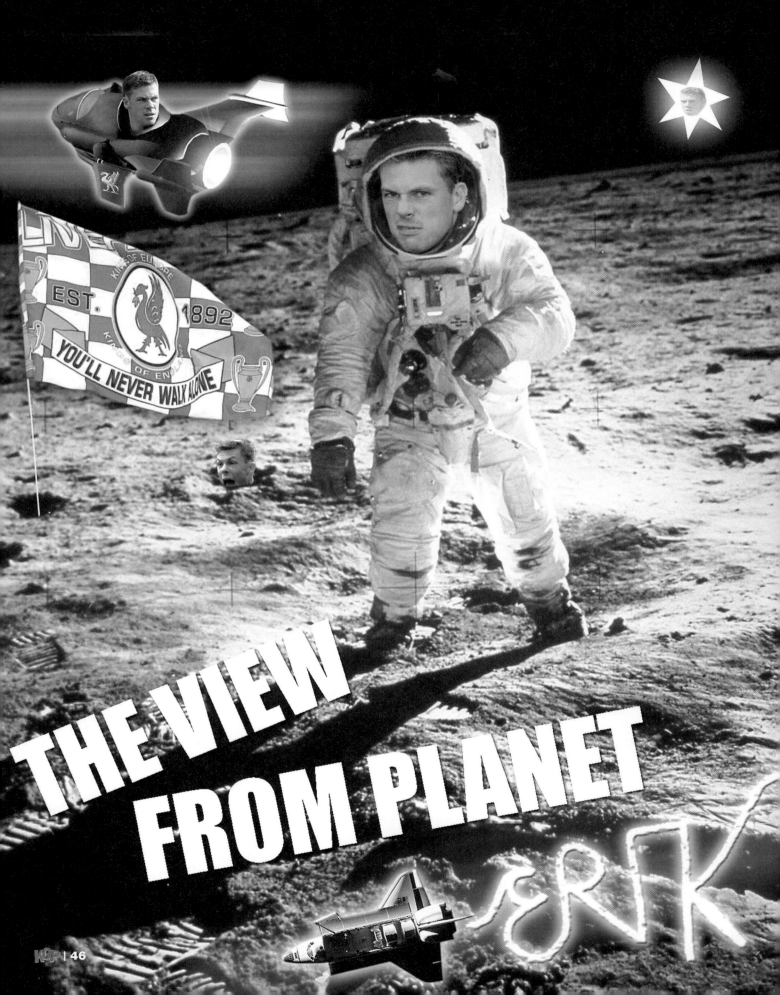

we've had many players who are out of this world but none to match a certain Erik Meijer. Every club should have one . . .

# THE VIEW FROM PLANET ERIK

## ERIK on fashion

"ITALY are always a force in football and they have some great players but that is not the reason for my interest.

"The reason is . . . their shirts.

"Let me explain. The Italians' shirts are made of a special material which stretches, supposedly making it more comfortable for the players to wear.

"And if you are comfortable you feel good, I know from experience that is true.

"When I was playing for Maastricht, about four or five of us tried this material during a season and we all found it beneficial. We even managed a draw away to the mighty Ajax, which was something we hadn't achieved for years.

"I think if you believe in something, such as the fabric of your shirt or the design of your boots, then it will have a positive effect. It's a psychological thing.

"I am sure that is why players these days wear boots that are coloured and not just black. If it makes you feel good then do it!"

## ERIK on making money from Jari

"LITMANEN bought my house in England and I made a nice surplus from the deal.

"It meant that at the end of the day, my stay in England didn't cost me anything!"

## ERIK on The Sami Hyypia Fish Dish (serves 2)

"I GOT the recipe from Sami's girlfriend. Sami has tried the food and he likes it so now it's your turn!"

INGREDIENTS

2 salmon steaks
1 big onion
142ml (or 5fl oz) of sour cream
Small potatoes (as many as required)
Broccoli
The juice of half a lemon
Half a glass of white wine

INSTRUCTIONS

Preheat the oven to 225 degrees. Put the salmon steaks on an oven-proof tray and squeeze the lemon juice over them. Cut the big onion into rings and put them over the fish. Add the sour cream on top and then, for the finishing touch, pour on the white wine. Cover the tray with aluminium foil and put in the oven for 25 minutes. Cook potatoes (normally 15-20 minutes). Boil broccoli for 5 mins.
**Erik's tip:** Use heated plates so the food stays warm longer and think of Sami when you are eating it!

## ERIK on Dortmund 2001

DESPITE leaving Liverpool, Erik's love for the club didn't die and he turned up to watch the 2001 UEFA Cup final against Alaves in Dortmund.

But unlike most footballers who prefer VIP treatment and go straight to the ground, Erik decided it was time to party with the travelling Kop.

He turned up in Dortmund's Alt Market wearing his old Liverpool shirt (it still had MEIJER 18 on the back) and a pair of LFC sunglasses.

Mad Erik then joined Kopites in having several pre-match bevvies and joining in a good old sing-song, even leading the singing of a couple of anti-Everton chants!

He later said: "I will never forget the day of the UEFA Cup final in Dortmund.

"I was in the square before the match. Apart from my wedding I haven't had such a great time!

"As soon as the fans saw me on that square I had to sing songs with them. It was an unbelievable atmosphere.

"The game itself was the most amazing one I have seen. In fact, it was the most perfect day all round."

## ERIK on Reserve commitment

ON one occasion, when Liverpool reserves were playing at St Helens' Knowsley Road ground, Erik was part of a team that were 4-0 up with just a couple of minutes to go.

Meijer chased down one full-back who passed the ball to his keeper. Meijer chased the keeper down – who gave the ball to his other full-back. Meijer then chased that full-back down and launched into a full-blooded tackle that took the ball out for a throw-in.

He promptly jumped to his feet and shook a clenched fist towards a crowd of about six men and a dog as if he'd just scored the winner in a cup final. That was Mad Erik for you.

**SEAN DUNDEE**

**FRANKIE SAYS ROLEX**

*Lampard's request to Roman for a bonus after he finds the net at Chelski*

By the time you read this I'll have been sent off

*Tim Cahill knows the rules every time he scores a goal now*

I @*!!#@! u on April 23 Loads of love Edye Rooney

*Rooney spots a face he remembers in the Old Trafford crowd*

ONCE A BLUE NOW A F*#T MANC

*Roonaldo impresses his new fans with a show of loyalty*

IF U ALL HATE SCOUSERS CLAP UR HANDS

*Gary Neville had to scrap this T-shirt because of a new team-mate*

**OFF TO A**

Lifting your shirt after a goal to show a message on a T-shirt is frowned upon these days. Here's a few that DIDN'T see the light of the day and avoided a red card!

I WENT TO PORTUGAL THIS SUMMER AND ALL I GOT WAS THIS LOUSY NO. 8 SHIRT

*Steven Gerrard decided against this one after getting handed Emile's old shirt*

**ARE YOUBL INDORSOME THINGARSENE???**

*One of the Arsenal players tests the dodgy eyesight of Arsene Wenger from the dugout*

ATTACK ATTACK ATTACK

*Gerard Houllier thought twice about giving this to one of his players last season*

You *!!,*@! SHOWER OF #!£!* *!!**e! *!!!

*Peter Reid gets the message across to his players in the dressing room*

1-0 TO THE ARSENAL

*Tony Adams was ready to unveil this message minutes before he went to pick up the FA Cup in 2001*

i'm lovin' it

*There were rumours that Mark Viduka had this lined up for his first Boro goal*

Bet you thought you'd never see this!

*Stephane Henchoz had this T-shirt ready for his long-awaited goal*

You never saw this!

*The Rob Jones goal that never came . . .*

*An England player celebrates yet another conquest under Sven*

# K TOP 10 Misses

Top o' the morning Kop-pickers! It's your favourite Anfield DJs Rushie and Spicey here ready to take a top-tastic tear-jerking stroll down memory lane. We do a lot of work for Liverpool and usually don't like to talk about it but as a special humongous one-off, let us present the all-time greatest ever in all history top 10 Anfield er, misses as voted by you the people that really matter – and we mean that most sincerely, folks . . .

## 10 RONNY HITS THE BAR
### v Aston Villa, April 1st 2002

Checkin' in at number 10, mate, is everybody's favourite oh, oh, Israelite Ronny Rosenthal with his chiller at Villa. Clean through in green he was at fault in front of the Holt End with a crossbartastic bonkers miss-and-a-half, mate.

## 9 ISTVAN KOZMA
### Hungaslavian Kop genius

In at nine, which he wasn't very often at Anfield, is that Hungaslavian wizard of the wing, Istvan Kozma. Rather than missin' chances, he just went missin, quite Lord Lucantabulous-literally. A Koptastic 45-minute performance against Chesterfield apart, he was so bad that if he'd been Greek he'd have been called Istvan Flopadopolus, mate.

## 8 ST MICHAEL'S DODGY PENS

### v Wimbledon, West Brom, Portsmouth, Roma, Basel etc

*The rain in Spain falls mainly on the plane and it'll be a Real ordeal if not-so-hot from the spot Owen takes a pen for the men from Madrid, mate. He may have been a goalmongous scoring machine for the Redmen but not so fabdiddilytabulous from 12-yards out.*

> Jamesie had me more nervous than a basket full of kittens on their way to the vet's mates!

## 7 DAVID JAMES

### Unsafest hands in soccer

*David James. Top bloke. Does a lotta work for charidy but doesn't like to talk about it so we will. In '97 he helped out those relegation threatened Sky Blues of Coventry with some flap-happy Nintendotastic goalkeeping. But good-old Jamo's charidy didn't stop there and he helped Manchesder Unided to the FA Premiership league championship title with some dodgy-dabulous cross-dodging keeping. Charidytastic, Kop-pickers.*

## 6 MEN IN TIGHTS

### Aka John Barnes . . .

*I can't think of anything as humongously awful, mate, as men wearing tights — except in a Robin-Hood-Bryan-Adams type of Hollywood way. Alan Barney Bonkers Rubble Kennedy might have had an excuse as he was wearing them for charidy panto, but what about that John Barnes? Digger's dodgy leg-warmers were part of his matchday winter wear and he'd even be spotted in gloves and a head-heating balaclava on a fridge-freezing January afternoon. Totally tightastic, boys and girls.*

# K TOP 10 Misses

## 5 KIT AND MISS

### The green away kit

A fashiontabulous faux-pas if ever there was one. Nevermind green around the fields of Anfield Road, Liverpool fans were green around the gills watching some horribilus away-day displays in a kit that made Jan Molby look like the jolly green giant and Torben look like Danish bacon gone off.

## 4 THE APPLIANCE OF SCIENCE

### The Anfield scoreboard

Climbing at four is the Anfield addition that puts the 'no' into technology. The clock stops so often that we're wondering if the bottomtastic-in-a-tight-yellow-boilersuit Anneka Rice is using it for a fantabulous new series of Treasure Hunt. Against Blackburn last season the scoreboard proclaimed in was 9-0. As Didi Hamann might tell you, nein, nein, nein!

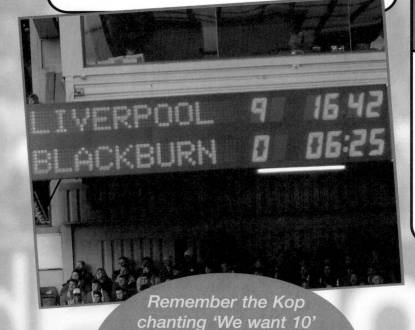

Remember the Kop chanting 'We want 10' mates? What a Kop-tabulous response to a quite goalmongous cock-up!

## 3 BLOND AMBITION

### Ant's blond braids

Hair today, gone tomorrow. To St Etienne. Definitely not a none mover this one. The bleachtastic blond look just wasn't enough for Anthony Le Tallec so he went and made the garlicmongous mistake of having braids put in. What a frogadabbadobulously bonkers thing to do that was, mate. Clearly the boy is an Oasis fan but while Noel Gallagher may have once sung you've gotta Corn Roll With It, he may have taken it a bit too literally.

**Tactics truck? More like the Loony Lorry. Wasn't exactly mullet-tastic was it, Jari?**

## 2 JARI ON THE TACTICS TRUCK

### Andy Townsend's TV nightmare

*Just beaten to the top spot was Andy Townsend's tacky tacticstastic truck, mate. As far as ITV innovations go it was an absolutely fabbadabulous way to lose viewers and we'll never forget the time the Finntastic Jari Litmanen joined Andy in his truck and smiled less than the audience at a Sportsmen's dinner with Paddy Crerand.*

## 1 LIVERPOOL LOU

### No 1 missus: Louise Redknapp

*Top of the Kop misses is the missus we'd all be over the moon to have as our own, mate, the toptottytastic Louise Redknapp. She's the type of gal who we like in a 'bring home to your mother' type of way and with Jamie inheriting his good looks from red-hot Harry, the Redknapps were always gonna be a match made in heaventabulous, er, heaven, mate.*

**The boy done good Spicey**

**Top of the Kops in anyone's book mate!**

## STAR CHRISTMAS BUY!!

Our unique Chelski game. See if you can solve the clues and find out who's guilty and who's innocent in the summer transfer mystery of the year. Who tried to tempt Stevie G to transfer mystery of the year. Who tried to tempt Stevie G to on in the airport departure lounge? And who was having a quiet word in the Liverpool skipper's ear in the England dressing room at Euro 2004? Play for yourself and find out if a crime against the Liver bird has been committed and if so, who dunnit?

**MASTER COLE**

**Stadium of Light dressing room**

**MRS. TERRY**

**Roman's ludicrously over-sized yacht**

SECRET PASSAGE

START

Chelski?

**PENTHOUSE**
CHELSEA VILLAGE

**Roman's not quite as ludicrously over-sized yacht**

**ROUBLES**
LOADS & LOADS OF

**England's Portuguese training camp**

START

Abramovich Airlines

**MR. BRIDGE**

SECRET PASSAGE

**Roman's private Boeing 767 Jet**

# Playing the game in your head

Football isn't an exact science but it gets you thinking. We stepped inside the minds of a Kopite as well as some teams, players and managers to see what it's all about . . .

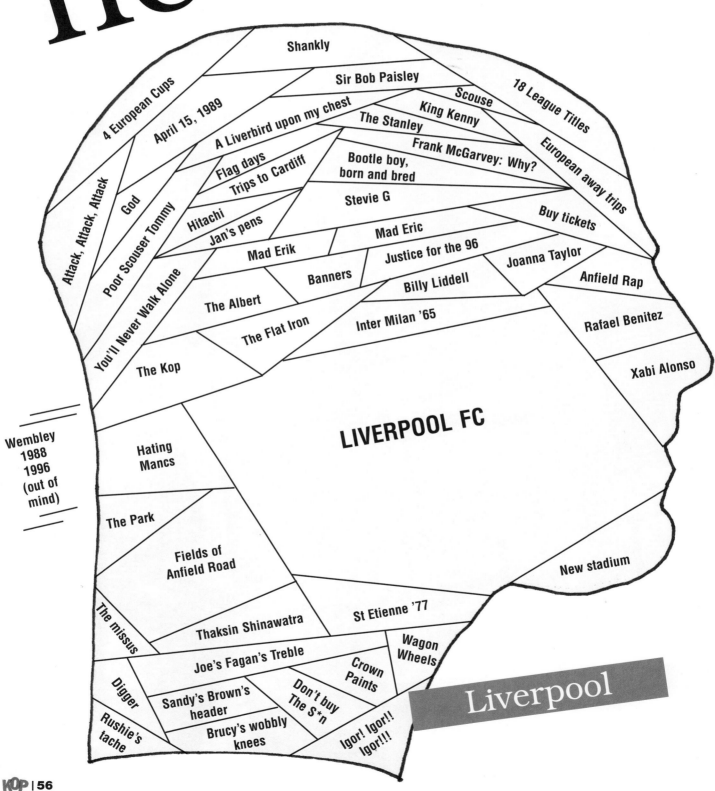

Shankly

Sir Bob Paisley

4 European Cups

April 15, 1989

A Liverbird upon my chest

Scouse

King Kenny

The Stanley

18 League Titles

Frank McGarvey: Why?

European away trips

Flag days

Trips to Cardiff

Bootle boy, born and bred

Attack, Attack, Attack

God

Poor Scouser Tommy

Hitachi

Jan's pens

Stevie G

Buy tickets

Mad Erik

Mad Eric

Justice for the 96

Joanna Taylor

Anfield Rap

You'll Never Walk Alone

The Albert

Banners

Billy Liddell

The Flat Iron

Inter Milan '65

Rafael Benitez

The Kop

Xabi Alonso

**LIVERPOOL FC**

Wembley
1988
1996
(out of
mind)

Hating
Mancs

The Park

Fields of
Anfield Road

New stadium

The missus

Thaksin Shinawatra

St Etienne '77

Wagon
Wheels

Joe's Fagan's Treble

Crown
Paints

Digger

Sandy's Brown's
header

Don't buy
The S*n

Rushie's
tache

Brucy's wobbly
knees

Igor! Igor!!
Igor!!!

**Liverpool**

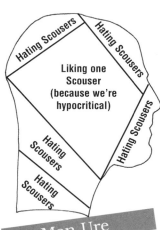

Hating Scousers • Hating Scousers • Liking one Scouser (because we're hypocritical) • Hating Scousers • Hating Scousers • Hating Scousers

**Man Ure**

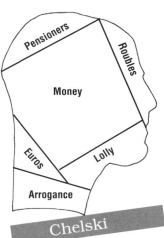

Pensioners • Roubles • Money • Euros • Lolly • Arrogance

**Chelski**

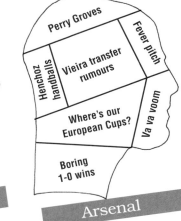

Perry Groves • Fever pitch • Henchoz handballs • Vieira transfer rumours • Va va voom • Where's our European Cups? • Boring 1-0 wins

**Arsenal**

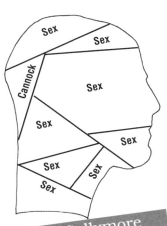

Sex • Sex • Cannock • Sex • Sex • Sex • Sex • Sex • Sex

**Stan Collymore**

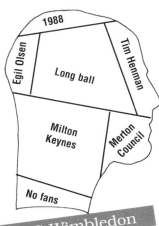

1988 • Egil Olsen • Tim Henman • Long ball • Milton Keynes • Merton Council • No fans

**AFC Wimbledon**

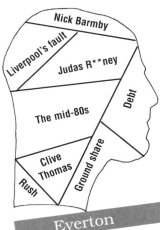

Nick Barmby • Liverpool's fault • Judas R**ney • Debt • The mid-80s • Clive Thomas • Ground share • Rush

**Everton**

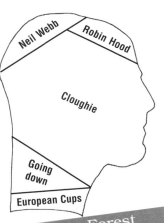

Neil Webb • Robin Hood • Cloughie • Going down • European Cups

**Notts Forest**

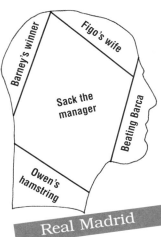

Barney's winner • Figo's wife • Sack the manager • Beating Barca • Owen's hamstring

**Real Madrid**

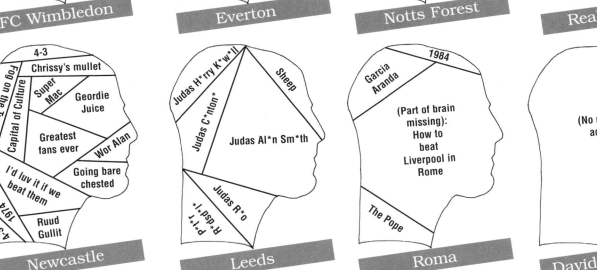

Newcastle head: 4-3 • Chrissy's mullet • Fog on the Tyne • Super Mac • Geordie Juice • Capital of Culture • Greatest fans ever • Wor Alan • I'd luv it if we beat them • Going bare chested • 1974 • 4-3 • Ruud Gullit

**Newcastle**

Leeds head: Judas H*rry K*w*ll • Sheep • Judas C*nton* • Judas Al*n Sm*th • Judas R*o • P*t*r R**dsd*l*

**Leeds**

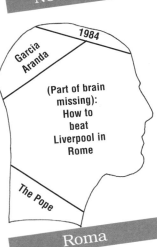

1984 • Garcia Aranda • (Part of brain missing): How to beat Liverpool in Rome • The Pope

**Roma**

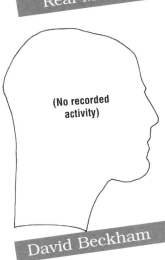

(No recorded activity)

**David Beckham**

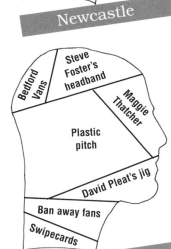

Steve Foster's headband • Bedford Vans • Maggie Thatcher • Plastic pitch • David Pleat's jig • Ban away fans • Swipecards

**Luton Town**

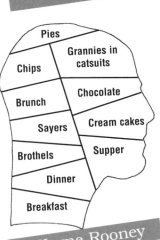

Pies • Grannies in catsuits • Chips • Chocolate • Brunch • Cream cakes • Sayers • Supper • Brothels • Dinner • Breakfast

**Wayne Rooney**

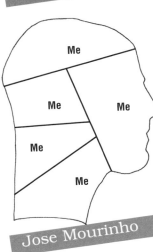

Me • Me • Me • Me • Me

**Jose Mourinho**

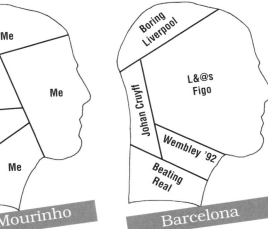

Boring Liverpool • L&@s Figo • Johan Cruyff • Wembley '92 • Beating Real

**Barcelona**

# The best of SPOTTED

**THE Kop Mole has got spies all over Liverpool and further afield. If there's a Redman out-and-about our Mole knows about it. Here's a few GENUINE sightings from over the past year!**

Former Liverpool midfielder **Michael Thomas** doing the security at the Radisson Hotel, Old Hall Street, while the Monaco team and Prince Albert were staying there.

**John Barnes** and his kids at Japanese restaurant Sapporo Teppanyaki on Duke Street.

**Josemi** looking fed up standing outside women's changing rooms in Zara, Liverpool City Centre.

**Jamie Carragher** pushing a pram in Cricket Menswear in Cavern Walks.

**Steve Finnan** on his mobile phone outside a portable toilet near The Strand during the Mathew Street Festival.

**Igor Biscan** and a friend talking loudly in Croatian about the Monaco game in the gym at the Radisson Hotel. Igor was later spotted heading into the beauty therapy area wearing just a towel!

**Robbie Fowler** enjoying a day of racing at Haydock Park.

**Kenny Dalglish** signing copies of 'Oh...I Am A Liverpudlian And I Come From The Spion Kop' outside the Kop magazine office.

**Ronnie Whelan** and a friend laughing as they came out of the Ace Place joke shop on Dale Street, Liverpool.

**Sami Hyypia** in the BMW garage on the corner of Leeds Street and Great Howard Street buying a car.

**Jamie Carragher** in the away end with the travelling Kop at the Riverside after travelling to the match on a Happy Al's coach.

**Djimi Traore** being shown around a flat at the Beetham Tower complex, Old Hall Street.

**Anthony Le Tallec, Florent Sinama-Pongolle, Djibril Cisse and Phillipe Mexes** in Baby Blue at the Albert Dock last Easter.

**John Barnes** ordering food at the McDonald's drive-thru near the Kings Dock.

**Kenny Dalglish, Paul Dalglish** and **Craig Phillips** from Big Brother at the Grand National, Aintree Racecourse.

Coldplay frontman **Chris Martin** watching Liverpool v Levski Sofia from the Main Stand.

**Graeme Souness** arguing with immigration officials at Washington Airport, USA.

*Day at the races: Robbie*

Ex-Red **Steve Harkness** flashing the cash at Zara one lunchtime.

**Stephane Henchoz** walking through the Pinewoods, Formby (not looking for Colleen McLoughlin's engagement ring!)

**Chris Kirkland** moving into his new £900,000 house in Aughton, near Ormskirk, and later spotted walking his Labrador in the local area and in the Spar shop near Town Green railway station.

*Pizza Hut: Vladi*

**Didi Hamann** struggling to park his Porsche in a tiny space on Old Hall Street, Liverpool.

**Chris Lawler** enjoying a bevvy in Rigby's on Dale Street, Liverpool.

Former Liverpool defender **Dominic Matteo** walking round alone in the ladieswear section in Harvey Nichols, Leeds.

**Florent Sinama-Pongolle** and his partner shopping in Tesco on Mather Avenue, Allerton.

Ex-Arsenal and Chelski midfielder **Emmanuel Petit** being given a guided tour of Melwood by his brother-in-law, **Bruno Cheyrou.**

**Steve Finnan** and **Steve Harkness** celebrating New Year's Eve 2003 in the Newz Bar, Water Street.

**Stephane Henchoz** buying a Sunday paper at the Esso petrol station on Liverpool Road, Crosby.

**Roy Evans** sitting on a wall outside the Stanley Gate pub, Bickerstaffe.

**Jamie Carragher** at a Fleetwood Mac concert with his mates in Manchester.

**Jon Otsemobor** shopping at designer clothes shop Open on Church Street.

**Rick Parry** asleep in the first class section of a British Airways flight from New York to Manchester.

**Sami Hyypia** and several players from Widnes RLFC in the sauna at the David Lloyd Fitness Centre, Speke.

**Vladimir Smicer** and his daughter outside Pizza Hut in Southport.

**Kenny Dalglish** leaving the Villa Romana Italian restaurant in Liverpool

**Jamie Carragher** having breakfast at Plumleys in Crosby.

**Michael Owen** and **Didi Hamann** having a coffee in Café Connect, Old Hall Street.

**Mark Lawrenson** puffing and panting his way through the Great North Run in Newcastle.

**Phil Thompson** happily posing for photos at the Merseyside Youth Games at the Bebington Oval, Wirral.

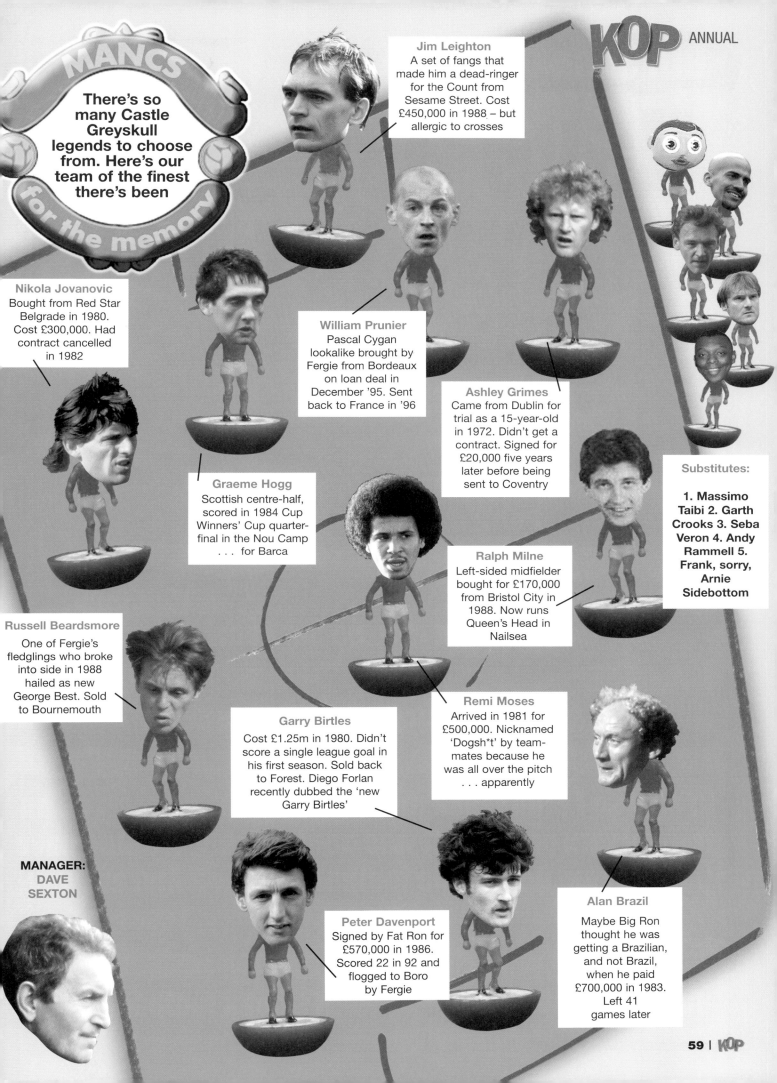

# MANCS for the memory

There's so many Castle Greyskull legends to choose from. Here's our team of the finest there's been

**Jim Leighton**
A set of fangs that made him a dead-ringer for the Count from Sesame Street. Cost £450,000 in 1988 – but allergic to crosses

**Nikola Jovanovic**
Bought from Red Star Belgrade in 1980. Cost £300,000. Had contract cancelled in 1982

**William Prunier**
Pascal Cygan lookalike brought by Fergie from Bordeaux on loan deal in December '95. Sent back to France in '96

**Ashley Grimes**
Came from Dublin for trial as a 15-year-old in 1972. Didn't get a contract. Signed for £20,000 five years later before being sent to Coventry

**Graeme Hogg**
Scottish centre-half, scored in 1984 Cup Winners' Cup quarter-final in the Nou Camp . . . for Barca

**Substitutes:**

1. Massimo Taibi 2. Garth Crooks 3. Seba Veron 4. Andy Rammell 5. Frank, sorry, Arnie Sidebottom

**Ralph Milne**
Left-sided midfielder bought for £170,000 from Bristol City in 1988. Now runs Queen's Head in Nailsea

**Russell Beardsmore**
One of Fergie's fledglings who broke into side in 1988 hailed as new George Best. Sold to Bournemouth

**Garry Birtles**
Cost £1.25m in 1980. Didn't score a single league goal in his first season. Sold back to Forest. Diego Forlan recently dubbed the 'new Garry Birtles'

**Remi Moses**
Arrived in 1981 for £500,000. Nicknamed 'Dogsh*t' by team-mates because he was all over the pitch . . . apparently

**MANAGER:**
DAVE SEXTON

**Peter Davenport**
Signed by Fat Ron for £570,000 in 1986. Scored 22 in 92 and flogged to Boro by Fergie

**Alan Brazil**
Maybe Big Ron thought he was getting a Brazilian, and not Brazil, when he paid £700,000 in 1983. Left 41 games later

## Bill Shankly's

# Have aye got news for yous

He was the master of the football quote, aye.
See if you can guess the blacked out words in
these classic Shankly soundbites . . .

(For answers, see opposite)

**Football is not a matter of ███████████ , it's more important than that**

**The trouble with ██████████████ is that they know the rules but they do not know the game**

**Although I'm a Scot, I'm proud to be called a ████**

**Of course I didn't take my wife to see ██████ as an anniversary present. It was her birthday. Would I have got married during the football season? And anyway, it wasn't ██████ , it was ███████ reserves**

**Anfield is a sort of a ████ it's not a football ground**

Yes. ███████ misses a few, but he gets in the right place to miss them

With Ron Yeats in defence, we could play ██████████ in goal

Barber asks Shanks a question: 'Anything off the top?' Shanks replies: 'Aye, ████████

I've been a ████████████. It follows you home, it follows you everywhere and eats into your family life

I would like to be remembered as a man who built up a family of people who could hold their heads up high and say ████████

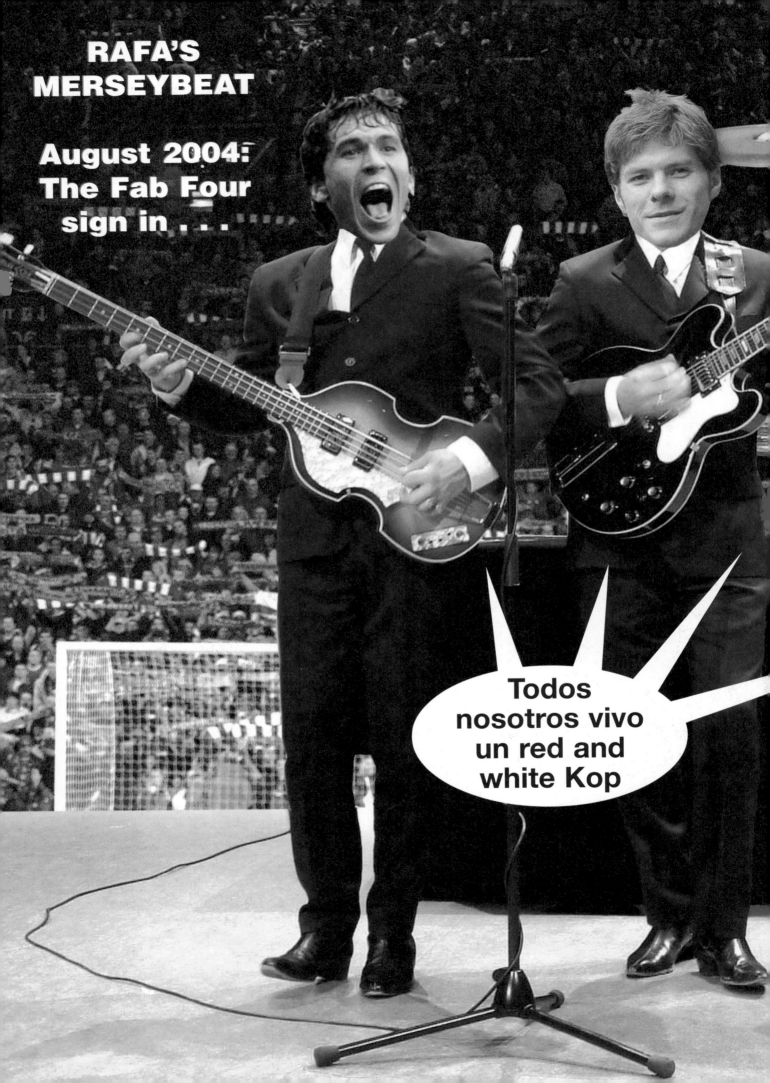